MW00618640

THE ELWAY YEARS

Inside the Super Bowl Era of the Denver Broncos

Mike Klis

TRIUMPH
BOOKS

Copyright © 2024 by Mike Klis

No part of this publication may be reproduced, stored in a retrieval system, or transmitted in any form by any means, electronic, mechanical, photocopying, or otherwise, without the prior written permission of the publisher, Triumph Books LLC, 814 North Franklin Street, Chicago, Illinois 60610.

Library of Congress Cataloging-in-Publication Data

Names: Klis, Mike.
Title: The Elway years: inside the Super Bowl era of the Denver Broncos / Mike Klis.
Description: Chicago, Illinois: Triumph Books, [2024] |
Identifiers: LCCN 2024025231 | ISBN 9781637276341 (cloth)
Subjects: LCSH: Elway, John, 1960- | Football players—United States—Biography. | Quarterbacks (Football)—United States—Biography. | Denver Broncos (Football team) | BISAC: SPORTS & RECREATION / Coaching / Football | TRAVEL / United States / West / Mountain (AZ, CO, ID, MT, NM, NV, UT, WY)
Classification: LCC GV939.E48 K55 2024 | DDC 796.332092 [B]—dc23/eng/20240606
LC record available at https://lccn.loc.gov/2024025231

This book is available in quantity at special discounts for your group or organization. For further information, contact:
Triumph Books LLC
814 North Franklin Street
Chicago, Illinois 60610
(312) 337-0747
www.triumphbooks.com

Printed in U.S.A.
ISBN: 978-1-63727-634-1
Design by Nord Compo
Photos courtesy of AP Images

*To my younger brothers, Tom and Bryan,
and sisters, Lori, Kathy, and Sherri*

CONTENTS

FOREWORD

I remember in 1980 watching the Oklahoma Sooners play the Stanford Cardinals (later changed to Cardinal) in Norman, Oklahoma. The Sooners were heavy favorites as they had won 20 in a row going back two seasons and were ranked No. 4 in the country. Stanford had a sophomore quarterback named John Elway.

John was the No. 1 high school prospect going into college. He had the ability to play both football and baseball. I had to watch this Oklahoma–Stanford game to see if this kid named Elway was really that good. I was about to find out. I knew how good Oklahoma was. I was expecting the Sooners to dominate. To my surprise, it was 31–0 Stanford in the middle of the third quarter. Elway's ability to escape the rush and make plays on his own made the Sooners look like an average team at best. It was so much fun to watch such a talented quarterback make so many unscheduled plays.

In 1982 I watched Elway come back against Ohio State in a game played in Columbus, Ohio. With about one minute, 30 seconds left, he found a way to go 80 yards for a touchdown to pull out a win. Five weeks later, Stanford, which was 4–3 at the time, beat No. 2-ranked Washington, which came into the game undefeated. John put up 43 points on Washington, and that win put Elway on the cover of *Sports Illustrated*.

I had never previously met John, but in January of 1984, I was hired by Dan Reeves, who was the Denver Broncos' head coach. I was excited to be in the pros. I was excited John Elway was our quarterback. His rookie year was in 1983, and he had his ups and downs, but the Broncos made the playoffs. From there he just got better and better.

John wound up being my closest friend during my first 15 years in the NFL. We took vacations together, worked out together, and golfed together. Our wives were very close, and John and I had the same goal: winning a Super Bowl. I was with John seven years as an assistant coach (1984–87, 1989–91), and we were together four years when I was a head coach (1995–98). Until you win a Super Bowl, you're always chasing a ghost. We finally caught the ghost and actually caught him twice.

I think you'll enjoy this book written by Mike Klis. I have known Mike since he moved from the Colorado Rockies beat to covering our team in 2005. We went 13–3 and hosted the AFC Championship Game that season. Mike and I respected each other. If you can understand that we both have jobs to do, then you've got a chance. Mike and I had that.

A central purpose of this book is to look back at John as the most influential person in Broncos' history. And there's really no question about that. I don't even think it's close. I mean, everyone knows what Terrell Davis did. What a player he was! And we had some other great players, too, Hall of Fame guys, but John went to five Super Bowls as a player and won two. Then as a general manager, he went to two and won one. The Broncos have been to eight Super Bowls. John was in the middle of seven of them, including all three world championships. There's really no question he's been the top figure in Broncos history. I was just glad I was able to be his coach for all those years and his friend to this day.

—*Mike Shanahan*

INTRODUCTION

When I was a kid, I played quarterback by myself in our backyard on Wolf Road, dropping back, rolling left, and throwing right like Archie Manning did, aiming at trees. I remember one period of my young life when I pretended to be Greg Cook, who was terrific for the Cincinnati Bengals in 1969 when he was the AFL Rookie of the Year. All those footballs pelted our trees. The goal, as a kid, was to be the high school quarterback.

But for all my dedication, I never quite made it. I was 6'0", 155. Lifting weights had just become a thing in the 1970s, and I was slow to catch on. Not strong enough. And I was always slow, no matter how many wind sprints I ran in the backyard.

I started at quarterback my junior year after the first-string guy, Tony Holler, suffered a shoulder injury that directed his sole focus to basketball and track. My stint didn't go well. In my senior year, I got benched after a couple starts. Actually, I had a couple practices where I thought I was all right. But come gametime—when 21 other guys were running every which way at full speed, and four of them were running directly at me—the event brought out the panic in me. I remember a couple times throwing the ball just to throw it because I didn't know what else to do.

I also played baseball and basketball as a kid and in high school. No one will ever convince me anything in sports is harder than playing quarterback. I believe my shortcomings at the position gave me a greater appreciation for anyone who played quarterback. I watch quarterbacks more intently, I'd like to think, than most observers. As a reporter I'd like to think I've been a little kinder to them. My first instinct is to not rip them when an interception is thrown—it's to look at why the interception occurred whether it be the pass rusher in his face, the receiver nudged off his route, the safety reading his keys.

And when a quarterback like John Elway comes along, my goodness do I watch him with awe. I remember watching Elway play on national TV his senior year at Stanford. No one had ever before or since thrown with more velocity. Elway would tell me a couple times over the years Brett Favre threw harder. The thing about both Elway and Favre is they put their whole derrière behind their throws. Nolan Ryan was the hardest thrower in baseball history, and if you watch his highlights, he delivered in such a way that he put his strong ass behind his pitches. Elway and Favre had strong asses, too, and they used it.

But Elway was first and he was also a strong runner, a terrific scrambler. To this day, one of the more mesmerizing feats of strength I've seen in sports is Elway scrambling left or right and throwing a pass shot out of bazooka to the far, opposite quadrant of the field to Vance Johnson. Elway was the most explosively talented quarterback I'd ever seen. Maybe not the most efficient—it wasn't until his 11th season of 1993 that Elway crossed the 60 percent completion rate. But if it was during the high time of a game, minutes to go, score or lose—when 21 other guys were running every which way at full speed, and four of them were running directly at him—Elway had the uncanny ability to put his remarkable skill set to good use.

Dan Marino was the better pure passer. Elway was a winner.

I have written several other historical Broncos books and thought I had done my last one when *The Denver Broncos All-Time All-Stars* was put to bed. But when presented with the opportunity to take on this project that focused on Elway and the Broncos' back-to-back Super Bowl championship seasons of 1997–98, I didn't hesitate. As a Broncos beat reporter—first for *The Denver Post*, then for 9NEWS—I had covered the entirety of Elway's 10-year reign as the team's general manager. He had a historically successful GM stint in the first five seasons of his term, only to oversee a disappointing final five seasons. I would describe our professional relationship as respectful at a stiff-armed distance.

We had a couple of candid conversations where he taught me so much about the game and its inner workings. There were a couple instances—the Elvis Dumervil fax fiasco and Von Miller contract negotiations come to mind—when my reporting got me a harshly-stated earful. So it goes. The uber-competitiveness Elway brought to fourth quarters as a quarterback was every bit still burning inside him as a GM. He just didn't have the avenue to release his competitiveness in those fourth quarters while viewing from up high in his executive box.

I mostly watched Elway the quarterback from my couch, though I would peek in as a newspaper sports reporter extra during his final three seasons of 1996–98. The Broncos were supposedly all about the Mastermind, coach Mike Shanahan, and running back Terrell Davis during that three-year period. But then Elway retired after the 1998 season, and a funny thing happened: the Broncos nosedived. It was a one-year crash at first, but it would be 15 more years—Peyton Manning's second in Denver—before the Broncos reached the Super Bowl again and 17 years before they won it all.

Between Elway the quarterback and Elway the GM, he led the Broncos to seven of their eight Super Bowl appearances and all three of their world championships. Elway by far is the most influential person in Broncos history. It was a privilege to recollect his journey.

CHAPTER ONE

THE FINAL BOW

At long last, John Elway was so *relaxed* leading up to The Big Game. For the fifth time in his marvelous career, Elway was the featured attraction at the No. 1 non-game event of the year—Super Bowl Media Day.

It was a Tuesday, January 26, 1999. Media Day was held at Pro Player Stadium in Miami, the same place Super Bowl XXXIII would be played five days later. But the setup had a different look. There was temporary flooring covering the grass field, and Elway—the biggest star in Colorado sports history, who based on his previous comments had one more game left in his fabulous career as the Denver Broncos' quarterback—was surrounded by hundreds of national reporters who crammed, elbowed, strained, and wondered.

As he sat in his high-rise chair before a horde of microphones, Elway was wearing hip shades, still another new version of a Broncos baseball cap, his all white with blue Nike swoosh XXXIII gameday uniform, and a comfortable demeanor. He smiled often with nary a squirm.

The Super Bowl Media Day gatherings had become like a leather helmet to Elway: older than the questions he was repeatedly asked. He was about to become the first quarterback in NFL history to start five Super Bowls. The reason Elway was sitting at ease, though, was because for the first time in his 16-year career he was sitting in his Media Day position as a Super Bowl-*winning* quarterback. On the wrong end of three Super Bowl blowouts—first against the New York Giants to cap the 1986 season, then the Washington Redskins (since renamed the Commanders) in 1987, and finally the 55–10 massacre from the San Francisco 49ers in 1989—Elway had finally, and determinedly, helicoptered the Broncos to a stunning, 31–24 upset win against the heavily favored Green Bay Packers the previous year to cap the 1997 season with the Super Bowl XXXII trophy.

That made Super Bowl XXXIII Media Day in Miami considerably more fun than the others. "It's been nice," Elway said as the seconds ticked down on his one-hour session. "It's a lot more pleasant in the fact that you're not talking about past Super Bowl failures all the time. I've got to tell you: from 1988 until we went last year, I answered the question whether my career could be complete without a Super Bowl victory a lot. It's been nice that I haven't had to answer that."

Though stated in various forms, the question that most confronted Elway during this Media Day session was whether he would retire after the Pro Bowl, which was to be played February 7 in Hawaii—a week after his Broncos would play against the Atlanta Falcons and his former head coach Dan

Reeves in Super Bowl XXXIII. Elway never directly answered the retirement questions during his Media Day session, instead offering hints each way. Returning for a 17th season and the opportunity to become the first quarterback to win three consecutive Super Bowls "does put a kink in the decision," he said, which could also mean that without the "kink" the decision was otherwise made, and he was headed straight for retirement. (Bart Starr did lead Green Bay to three consecutive NFL titles from 1965 to 1967. The first Super Bowl, however, wasn't played until after the 1966 season. So Starr gets credit for back-to-back Super Bowls but not the 1965 NFL championship, at least not in the *Super Bowl era*, which is silly, but there you go.) "Let me say this: I never want to retire," Elway said on that early 1999 day in Miami. "I know in my mind I'll always miss the game, and it'll be a tough day when I do have to say that I'm not going to play anymore. I know physically it just gets tougher and tougher every year and I'd like to be able to chase my kids when I do retire. I don't want to crawl away."

Elway's body language, though, was of a man who knew the end was but one Big Game away. No question bothered him no matter how personal or ill-mannered it was stated. He was 38 years old, and no human body was meant to play football that long, at least not one who took the physical punishment Elway did as a scrambler, the type of scrambler

5

who given a choice of sliding safely a yard short of the first down or taking the hit if it meant moving the chains never failed to absorb the blow.

* * *

Twenty-five years later, Elway was sitting at a table in the Perfect Landing restaurant, overlooking private jets that would take off and land at the Centennial Airport. Not far away, Elway's own private jet was awaiting takeoff to Las Vegas, where he and some friends had a guys' trip planned that included watching the Formula 1 Las Vegas Grand Prix. If the mood struck the group to hit the tables, so be it. Then it was on to Palm Desert for a round of golf. Maybe back for the Denver Broncos game Sunday night against the Minnesota Vikings at Empower Field at Mile High, The House Elway and the 1997–98 Broncos Built.

At 63 years old, time was on Elway's side. Wearing a quarter-zipped pullover and that famously big Elway smile as he walked in and turned heads, Elway was every bit as comfortable as he was 25 years earlier on what would be his final Super Bowl Media Day as a player. He would attend two more Super Bowl Media Day sessions as the Broncos' general manager following the 2013 and 2015 seasons. But now as he sat down to discuss where his mind was in the days leading up to Super Bowl XXXIII, Elway was nearly three years removed from his final season as Broncos general manager, which was in 2020. He had lost all the stress and pounds the football executive job had slowly put on him during his 10-year term.

As he recollected his final days as a player, the days leading up to Super Bowl XXXIII, Elway viewed much of it, though, through an executive's lens. "Yeah, I think I knew it was probably my last game," Elway said before his plate of chiles rellenos and eggs arrived. "I didn't really want to think about that, though. I wanted to get time to get away from it and not think about it in the middle of it. Here's the thing about that game: we knew we were much better than they were. And all we had to do was go play like were capable of, and if we do, then we'll win, which was not the case in the other Super Bowls. [Against] the Pack we were 13-point underdogs, they were the world champs. But we were so good that last year; we had that one hiccup in New York and then we went down to Miami, and it didn't matter. And then we came back and played great against Seattle and the players— we didn't play great in the AFC Championship Game until the second half. But it was really we knew we were better."

That's another reason why Elway was so relaxed as addressed the Super Bowl XXXIII media throng. "My biggest concern was rain," Elway said. "It was like 50-50. It poured about 30 minutes after. The rain would have equalized things. And that whole week Dan was saying Terrell was not going to beat us, right? So that's where Mike had a great plan. We spread 'em out and threw it all over."

* * *

After John Elway threw for 336 yards in that Super Bowl XXXIII—80 of which came on a roll-right, throw-back launch down the left seam to post-running Rod Smith for a touchdown, a heave that perfectly personified Elway's career—in a 34–19 win against the Atlanta Falcons, he was awarded the Super Bowl XXXIII MVP. And then Elway did hang 'em up. "I was 95 percent there," Elway said later when asked what the truth was about his retirement as he participated in the Super Bowl XXXIII Media Day. "If I hadn't got banged up that year—I tore that hamstring and I fell on the ball and hurt my ribs, missed four games—I might have come back if I hadn't had those deals. But I was getting to the point where after you had won two, three would be great, but you've answered the questions you needed to answer."

Did he ever. Elway went from hearing how he couldn't win the Big One for at least a decade of his career to amending the sports cliché from "going out on top" to "going out like Elway." Every single elite athlete with a touch of an imagination dreams of not only having a Hall of Fame career, but also taking a bow and hearing the applause at the absolute final moment of that person's career.

Elway accomplished both. He was a first-ballot Pro Football Hall of Famer, which is the top individual honor at the national level. Locally, Broncos owner Pat Bowlen may have outdone the Pro Football Hall of Fame by waving the mandatory five-year waiting period so Elway could be immediately inducted into the team's Ring of Fame in the fall of 1999. And Elway would also not only go out as a champion, but also a back-to-back champion. Old Western double features with John Wayne as the headliner didn't come up with scripts like that. They couldn't. They had to make the movies somewhat believable.

"This one's for John!" were the four words Bowlen said immediately after the team owner was handed the first Lombardi Trophy in Denver Broncos history on January 25, 1998 on the Super Bowl XXXII stage rolled out at Qualcomm Stadium in San Diego. Laced within all the quality characteristics Bowlen had as an owner—a competitive fortitude that helped produce more Super Bowl appearances (six) than losing seasons (five) during his 30-year reign—was a shyness that made him uncomfortable on a national stage, no matter how pleasant the circumstances.

Quickly moving the spotlight to his quarterback was Bowlen's way of hurriedly getting out of the way. The truth is Elway didn't play all that well in Super Bowl XXXII, at least not as a passer. He did deliver the game's most inspirational play with his eight-yard helicopter scramble that converted a third and 6 to set up a first and goal and Terrell Davis' go-ahead touchdown. But overall it seemed those three previous Super Bowl blowout defeats were constricting Elway the passer. He finished just 12-of-22 passing for 123 yards with no touchdowns and one interception. The pick came four plays after the helicopter, and that interception cost the Broncos a chance to go up 14 points in the final seconds of the third quarter. His 51.9 passer rating in Super Bowl XXXII was the fourth worst of his 22 playoff games.

He played much better in his first Super Bowl, which was Super Bowl XXI against the New York Giants to cap the 1986 season. Coming off his famed "Drive" to beat the Cleveland Browns in the 1986 AFC Championship Game, Elway two weeks later in the Super Bowl threw for 304 yards and a touchdown against the Giants while completing 22-of-37 passes. But because the Broncos lost 39–20, Elway's performance in his first Big Game got folded into the next two Super Bowl blowouts to the Washington Redskins and San Francisco 49ers.

Three Super Bowl losses in a row by a combined 96 points became, "Yeah, Elway is great, but he can't win the Big One." "We have first and goal at the one and we run a quarterback roll right where we don't block Lawrence Taylor on the backside," Elway said in recapping his first three Super Bowl defeats in chronological order. "And then the second half, Phil Simms was on fire. We couldn't stop him. Then you go against Washington, and we're up 10–0 and 19 plays later we're down 35–10. [Washington left tackle] Joe Jacoby would have run for 150 yards. [Against the] Niners we never had a chance. That is a team that's not mentioned as one of the all-time best, but they were in my mind. They don't get talked about that way."

But win the Big One, as he and the Broncos did in surprise fashion against the Green Bay Packers, and it didn't matter how much Elway struggled to find his throwing rhythm in the game. There was that spectacular, balletic rhythm as he went airborne between three Green Bay defenders to take a high/low blast that sent him spinning sideways forward from right to rear. Elway had made a sacrificial body leap two yards past the first down stick, which changed what would have been a chip-shot field goal attempt for Jason Elam to extending a drive that became a Terrell Davis touchdown. Stats don't matter next to victory. Elway had done enough to help his team win.

Because the Broncos would go on to beat the Packers, all anyone remembers about Elway from Super Bowl XXXII was the helicopter. It stamped both Elway's tremendous off-script ability and his dogged competitiveness. "Funny how those things work out that way," Elway said with his wide smile.

Although retirement was a possibility after that Super Bowl XXXII win, there would be one more season for Elway. It was the easiest season the Broncos ever had in their now 64-season history—but one of the toughest for Elway. They were 8–0 halfway through the 1998 season as six-county Denver metropolitan voters on the first Tuesday of November approved the continuation of a .1 percent Coors Field sales tax that was to fund 75 percent of a new Broncos stadium. They went 13–0 and clinched the AFC's No. 1 playoff seed before they stumbled for two weeks at the New York Giants and at the Miami Dolphins, but they reclaimed their dominant play by helping Davis become only the fourth player in NFL history to surpass 2,000 yards to become the league's MVP. The Broncos then cruised through their two AFC postseason opponents—the Dolphins and New York Jets—by a combined 48 points before going up 31–6 in the fourth quarter against the Falcons in Super Bowl XXXIII.

But even if the 1998 Broncos were easily the best team in franchise history, it wasn't the easiest season for Elway. He essentially missed five games because of two injuries—an aggravated hamstring strain (a softer word for "tear") early in the season and battered ribs late—and the Broncos behind backup quarterback Bubby Brister won all five. While Elway had the most efficient passing season of his career, posting a single season-best 93.2 passer rating and earning his ninth Pro Bowl berth, he ran for a career-low 94 yards on 2.5 yards per carry and he took the last of his then-NFL-record 516 sacks. Elway was still great. But it almost hurt to watch his pigeon-toed walk move so gingerly between snaps on the football field. "I'm a better quarterback and a better passer than I ever have been," Elway had said in 1997. "What I'd like to be is 37 in my 27-year-old body."

It's difficult to remember now, but when Elway retired, he was in the conversation for *the* greatest quarterback in NFL history. He generally finished second in those arguments to Joe Montana, who was exquisite in all four Super Bowl games he played in and won. Montana threw 11 touchdown passes against 0 interceptions while going 4–0 in Super Bowls. No one will ever exceed him as the greatest quarterback in Super Bowl history, not even Tom Brady and his 7–3 record in the Big Game.

But after Elway was running well behind fellow 1983 draftmate Dan Marino on the top quarterback lists early in his career, Elway's legacy had surpassed that of the Dolphins' passing great. Marino may have been a better pure passer in terms of accuracy and quarterback rating, but Elway was the bigger winner. And as Peyton Manning discovered in a later generation comparison to Brady, Super Bowls are what most defines a quarterback. Brady was to Manning what Elway was to Marino. "I personally feel John's the GOAT," said defensive linemen Mike Lodish, whose six Super Bowl games were a record until Brady came along. "And that's not because I played alongside him or had the pleasure of being associated with him. He's the guy who closed two deals, went to five. He had solid teams when he went to the Super Bowls before, but I remember watching him when I was growing up. You give him a couple more pieces of ammunition, he has six rings, maybe seven rings. Who knows?"

One of the best compliments Dan Reeves paid to his former quarterback came while he was paying tribute to his former Atlanta Falcons kicker Morten Andersen. "Morten is one of those guys who, if it's 38–37, he's at his best," Reeves said prior to Andersen's Pro Football Hall of Fame induction in 2017. "He's like Michael Jordan or John Elway. When there's two minutes to go and the game is on the line, he's better in that situation than if there's no pressure."

When Elway called it a career after 16 seasons, his statistics were impressive, but they would become partially swallowed up over time as the NFL evolved into a more passer-friendly game. He was No. 2 with 51,475 yards at the time of his retirement but now ranks 12th. He was No. 3 with exactly 300 touchdown passes but now ranks 14th. His 79.9 career passer rating ranked 25th at the time of his retirement and 94th 25 years later.

Where Elway was No. 1 at the time of his retirement—and is still among the best today—is in the winning categories. He was the all-time leader with 148 regular-season wins and is still sixth. His 47 fourth-quarter/overtime game-winning or game-tying drives were the most by a quarterback upon his retirement and is still among the top five today. He was the NFL's MVP in the 1987 regular season and Super Bowl MVP in XXXIII to cap 1998. And most importantly, Elway's five Super Bowl appearances were the most by any quarterback at the time of his retirement and surpassed only by Brady's 10 since.

The Broncos have been one of the winningest franchises in NFL history largely because they had one of the top two or three clutch quarterbacks of all time. It was Elway who delivered the Broncos to prominence. "We absolutely do not win two Super Bowls without John Elway," said Ed McCaffrey, a starting receiver on the Broncos' 1997–98, back-to-back Super Bowl teams. "In the front office he went on to win another one. He has meant so much to this organization as one of the greatest players to ever playing in the history of the NFL and certainly the greatest player in Broncos history. But then he topped it by going into the front office and helping to bring Peyton Manning to Denver and winning another Super Bowl. His impact has been monumental."

No one person had a greater influence, or was more influential, on the Broncos' now 65-year history than Elway. "Oh God, dang, it's not even close," said Gary Kubiak, Elway's longtime backup quarterback, offensive coordinator, and later head coach hired by Elway, the GM. "Holy [heck], when you think about how long he played—the thing I always tell people: the thing I'm most amazed by is how long he stayed in the game until his team got good enough to award him with some championships. You think of everything he went through: losing the three Super Bowls, all of that scrutiny he had to contend with, and all those things, and all the sudden, it was, what, Year 15, we're good enough to win Super Bowls. Not many guys stay in the fight that long, just a credit to who he is. And then he goes in there and what he did as a general manager with that team was incredible. The run they went on there and the success they had with the moves and decisions he made—there's no argument for what one guy did for one franchise for that length of time in various roles. It will probably never be matched again."

CHAPTER TWO

THE ARRIVAL

L ooking back upon John Elway's arrival in Denver, one would expect a Denver Broncos player or three would recall some resentment. Something along the lines of, "What a spoiled kid. He didn't want to play for Baltimore so he took his ball and went to Denver." That was insinuated by Pittsburgh Steelers four-time-winning Super Bowl quarterback Terry Bradshaw, Elway's harshest critic from that time.

"I'd be willing to bet you ran into none of that," he said. Tom Jackson was one of the Broncos' biggest stars at the time and one of several Orange Crush defenders who were on the back end of their careers when Elway arrived.

Jackson was correct. None of the several veterans interviewed remembered envy or jealousy of Elway. Zero. Zip. That's saying something because arguably the most overlooked group of players in NFL history were the Orange Crush defenders from the Broncos' magical 1977 season. Even today, nearly 50 years later, only one player from that iconic Orange Crush defense has been elected into the Pro Football Hall of Fame. Randy Gradishar, an inside linebacker from that famed Broncos defense, finally received formal election in

February 2024. But it took half a century for one of the best defensive units in NFL history to finally get its first Bronze Bust. "We were so desperate for a quarterback who would give us a chance to accomplish the things we thought we should be doing that when John came along, all of us thought we had been gifted this great young quarterback," Jackson said. "A lot of our [Orange Crush] guys were leaving, on the verge of leaving. Billy had retired. Really, our true leader was Billy Thompson. But we were grateful to have John. And even though he got all that attention and it was simply natural that it came his way, he was very unassuming when he was with us. Film sessions that he would invite us to because they were going to have a little beer, John would say, 'You guys want to come on over and hang with us a little bit?' Yes, yes we want to do that. So even though he was a superstar and the first real superstar for us on our team—Floyd Little was with the team when I joined—but there was a different status that John brought."

By the time the kid arrived on an otherwise veteran-laden Broncos team in 1983, he had already figured out how to acclimate himself in a new environment. "The thing is it was kind of the third time I'd been through that," Elway said over breakfast in mid-November 2023. "The first time I went through it was when we moved from Pullman, Washington, to Granada Hills [Los Angeles]. I was a ninth grader going into

10th grade. My dad was head coach at Cal-State Northridge, which was in the city right next to where I went to high school at Granada Hills.

"So I was coming down there, and the rumor was the next Joe Namath was coming down from Washington. And all I had ever run was the single wing. And this high school was throwing the ball all over the place, and I had done none of that. I played basketball and baseball, but football was like third on the list. So I walked in there, and they're all looking at me…and they had two junior quarterbacks so that's the first time I felt it. I was always trying to adjust in high school. I did that, and that was the first time and then I went to Stanford and went through it there as one of the top recruits. So I had gone through it before. What I learned was: if I played well, that other stuff would go away."

Thompson, the strong safety, had retired two years prior to Elway's arrival. Gradishar would play one more season, Elway's rookie year, before hanging them up. Barney Chavous, the underrated 3-4 defensive end, retired rather than take a backup role during the 1986 training camp. Four other Orange Crush starters—Steve Foley, Rubin Carter, Louis Wright, and Jackson—would retire from their decade-plus playing careers after the 1986 season, the year Elway's career broke out with The Drive. "We never had that quarterback position sewed up. It was like Denver was looking for water, and all the sudden, we found the oasis when John came," Chavous said with a laugh. "Our class—Rubin, Tom, Louis—we had never won the Super Bowl. When we got John, I called him 'my hero.' I did call him that. And then he called me his hero, and we'd go back and forth."

John Albert Elway Jr. was traded from the Baltimore Colts to the Broncos on May 2, 1983, in what to that point was easily the biggest trade in NFL history. The impetus for the trade was: one, Elway was the greatest quarterback prospect ever to come out of college. Ever. Not before or since has there been a quarterback with a near tight end-sized frame, Nolan Ryan arm strength, and Bobby Douglass-type scrambling and running ability. Sure, Peyton Manning had the pedigree and size. But he didn't come close to having Elway's arm strength or mobility. Call Manning, the No. 1 overall selection in 1998, the second best quarterback prospect of all time. "In all my playing days and since, when they talk about somebody's superior arm strength, John Elway had *the* strongest arm," said Foley, a Broncos starting safety through the first four seasons of Elway's NFL career. "It was painful to block a pass. I was playing corner and guarding somebody in practice. And if you weren't in position in front, you didn't make up one step on an out route. You didn't make up anything. If you were there and in perfect position and out in front, you could maybe hit it out of a receiver's hands, but if you were just a shade behind, you're not making it up. Nobody threw with as much velocity as John did. Nobody. Not Bradshaw, not Bert Jones. They just didn't throw the ball like that. He put his whole body into it."

And two, the trade came about because Elway refused to play for the Colts. Not the Colts, per se, but their owner Robert Irsay and head coach Frank Kush. Elway made it clear well before the NFL draft he didn't want to play for the Colts, but their general manager, Ernie Accorsi, took him with the No. 1 overall draft pick anyway, saying he wasn't going to pass on such a once-in-a-lifetime talent while on his watch. Problem was the Colts weren't on Accorsi's watch. That belonged to Irsay and Kush. Elway, strongly influenced by his father, Jack, wanted no part of playing for Irsay or Kush. Jack Elway was a longtime college coach who went up against Kush when the latter was a longtime head coach of the Arizona State Sun Devils. Kush was not only known as a taskmaster, but also his methods today would have been deemed abusive. For that day, too. He was eventually fired from Arizona State in 1979 for allegedly punching a punter, then trying to cover up the incident.

That was not Jack Elway's style of coaching, and he didn't want his son John subjected to such demeaning methods. There was also the matter of Irsay's erratic behavior. There always seemed to be unwanted drama surrounding the Colts owner whether it was feuding with the city of Baltimore over the use of their antiquated stadium or the gambling problems of quarterback Art Schlichter, the team's first-round draft pick in 1982. Schlichter's dramatic fall from grace was why the Colts had the No. 1 overall pick and again needed a quarterback in 1983. It was also no secret that Irsay was a heavy drinker, and all these issues gave Jack Elway and his coveted son good reason to want to play anywhere in the NFL but Baltimore.

Still, Accorsi drafted him, passing on the other first-round quarterback likes of Jim Kelly, Dan Marino, Tony Eason, Todd Blackledge, and Ken O'Brien in a 1983 NFL Draft that was widely dubbed "The Year of the Quarterback." Elway was announced as the No. 1 overall pick of the Colts on April 26, 1983, and six days would pass before he was traded to the Broncos. In between was a press conference, in which Elway on the advice of his agent, Marvin Demoff, said he would prefer to stay on the West Coast. Demoff later regretted this tactic as it backfired on Elway, and Bradshaw ripped the top draft pick as a spoiled brat. "For Elway to say I want to be on the West Coast, I'm a California boy...well, who cares who you are?" Bradshaw said in a 1983 interview that was replayed years later on ESPN's *30 for 30: Elway to Marino* documentary. "And he said, 'I'll play baseball.' Well, then play baseball. You should play baseball because in my opinion he's not the kind of guy you win championships with."

The previous year, after his junior season at Stanford, Elway had been a second-round draft pick of Major League Baseball's New York Yankees and played right field for their Class A minor league team in the summer of 1982. It was Yankees owner George Steinbrenner who ordered his baseball people to select Elway, a left-handed hitter with decent speed, some power, and, of course, a cannon right arm. Steinbrenner's authority meant there was little doubt Elway would one day wear pinstripes at famed Yankee Stadium. Steinbrenner would see to it. And so would Elway's natural baseball's talent. So unlike other No. 1 overall NFL draft picks, Elway had another option. And he threatened to use it. Elway said he would return to the minor leagues to continue his baseball pursuit with the Yankees. He hit .318 with four homers and 13 stolen bases in 42 games for Class A Oneonta in 1982 so baseball was no idle threat.

But then Broncos owner Edgar Kaiser Jr. worked over Irsay for a trade. The Broncos sent their No. 4 overall draft pick, which happened to be Northwestern left tackle Chris Hinton, quarterback Mark Herrmann, and the following year's No. 1 draft pick that turned out to be Ron Solt, who became a 10-year starting right guard who made one Pro Bowl, to the Colts in exchange for Elway. Such a trade today would have meant the Broncos giving up at least two first-round draft picks and two second-round picks, but it was Elway's successful career that wound up driving the trade price up for a franchise-type quarterback. "It was a surprise I ended up there because they had no interest at the start," Elway said of the Broncos.

The trade was consummated so late in the night on May 2 that there was a late-into-the-night press conference. "A lot of the drama we were unaware of," Jackson said. "I was aware he was the first overall pick in the draft. I knew that he vaguely didn't want to play for Baltimore. But the drama of the situation…a basketball game is going on, and I get a call from Billy Thompson, who's at the game. And Billy tells me we're getting John Elway. And I go, 'Yeah, right.' And he goes, 'No, I think it's a done deal.' I think Dan [Reeves] was there at the game, and that was the connection to how it was heard. But the drama that led up to that moment, I watched the 30 for 30 on ESPN that has told me the story, but at the time I was not aware of all the things that went on behind the scenes."

The basketball game to which Jackson refers was an NBA second-round playoff between the Denver Nuggets against the San Antonio Spurs. The Nuggets behind Kiki Vandeweghe's 37 points beat George Gervin's Spurs 124–114 in what turned out to be Denver's last game of the season at since demolished

McNichols Arena. As the Nuggets staved off elimination for one more game, word spread through the arena the Broncos had just inconceivably finished off the trade for Elway.

Other teammates from that 1983 team verified Jackson's account. Remember it was a different time. There wasn't the Internet—let alone Twitter or X, Instagram, or other instantaneous social media avenues of communication. "I didn't know anything about all that controversy," said Ken Lanier, who would be the Broncos' starting right tackle the first 10 years of Elway's career. "I was happy we drafted Chris Hinton. I figured he would really solidify our offensive line. But when we traded Hinton for Elway, I remember thinking, *All right. Here we go.*"

Chavous was a longtime defensive end and Broncos coach whose 25 years with the Broncos spanned before and after Elway. "Yeah, I remember it," he said. "We couldn't believe it. We had drafted Chris Hinton at offensive tackle. I figured at the time we had [quarterbacks] DeBerg and Herrmann, and one of our big problems was we needed better protection. So when we drafted Hinton, we had hope. But then I heard we got Elway and I remembered when I was hunting at Red Olson's place. I had never seen John play before. I was sitting down eating, and Stanford was playing. I think it was against Cal. I forgot who they were playing. Anyway, I was sitting there eating and I saw John scramble out of the pocket, and he threw the ball and he got my attention. I looked at Red and said, 'That's a quarterback. That's the kind of guy we need right there.' So when John got to Denver, I told him about that. He remembered the game and the play and everything. As a rookie coming in, we had a bunch of vets on the team. And usually rookies have to prove themselves. But when John came in, all us older guys had our eyes wide open. We opened our arms for him, and he opened his arms to us, and then Tom and all of us starting calling him 'hero.'"

Steve Watson had been the Broncos' leading receiver the previous two years for Craig Morton in 1981 and Steve DeBerg, Herrmann, and Morton in the strike-shortened season of 1982. Watson remained the No. 1 receiver through Elway's first four seasons and then made way for the Broncos' famed Three Amigos of Vance Johnson, Mark Jackson, and Ricky Nattiel. "Every year it was, 'Who are we going to draft to replace me?'" Watson said when asked of his reaction to the Elway trade. "That's the way I always looked at it. But when the Elway deal came down, I didn't think a whole lot of it. I think I had just finished with Craig Morton, and we had DeBerg. And [Gary] Kubiak came [as an eighth-round draft pick in 1983] with John. We were still trying to figure out this Dan Reeves guy, our new coach. I was more worried about my own job than whoever else was coming in. I just worked on trying to be the best I could be."

Kubiak was a consummate professional as a backup quarterback, a quarterbacks coach, offensive coordinator, head coach, and senior personnel advisor through his nearly 40 seasons in the NFL. But he couldn't have been doing backflips when he first learned Elway was traded to his team. He quickly gained empathy for his new teammate, though, when he saw how Elway was so overwhelmed with fan and media attention. "I was drafted by the Broncos and I think it was about a week later when they made the big trade for John," Kubiak said. "I had just become part of the team so we came in on 58th Avenue together many, many years ago."

Soon enough, Kubiak fell into a role as Elway's closest confidant. They were in meetings together, went to dinner together, hung out in dorm rooms together during training camp. "First of all, from a player's standpoint, being a quarterback, it was intimidating," Kubiak said. "Here I got drafted, and we go to practice, and I watch him and I'm like, 'Oh my God, this is what it takes to play in this league?' He's so talented. A big, good-looking athlete, a powerful arm, and then every day throwing next to him, I'd go back to my room and thinking, *Man, I don't know if I can do this. I can't do anything that guy can do.* So that was very intimidating. But to see the status, what he had to go through, there wasn't social media stuff, but back then I think he was the start of where they followed him doing everything—where he got

a haircut, whatever he did. I think they called it the Elway
Watch. But to see the attention he was under each and every
day and becoming the face of that franchise with Mr. Bowlen
having just bought the team, so I just sat there witnessing
the whole thing."

Elway struggled mightily his rookie season. Although
the Broncos finished with an encouraging 9–7 record, they
were 4–6 in Elway's starts. He threw 14 interceptions against
just seven touchdown passes. Often he was benched in favor
of DeBerg. Then again, it's difficult to perform when you're
young and suffocated. Elway would later tell Rick Reilly of
Sports Illustrated he felt like he was living in a fish bowl
thanks to Denver's highly competitive, near-century long,
two-newspaper market while sports talk radio was just starting
to grab drive-time listeners. "When John came in, *The Denver
Post* and the *Rocky Mountain News* were both going full steam
ahead," Watson said. "*The Post* and *Rocky* were banging heads.
It was nonstop. The Elway Watch. If it wasn't what was he
giving out on Halloween, then it was how much was he tip-
ping. It was everything, everywhere. He was under a micro-
scope, for sure. But when he was with us and when he was
in the huddle, we were a team. It was fun. Running down
the field, I would run my route, but if I had to do something
different, I'd do it. It was fun."

"I remember the time I saw him get escorted out of the stadium by the police," Jackson said. "Just watching him leave the stadium and having police around him as he was going to his car, and I thought, *My God*. He's all of that. He's this star. He's the star of the team. He's going to be the catalyst for whatever happens to this organization, and it's going to be good because I've not seen anyone more talented than he was. I had not seen anyone who could throw and quite frankly, when I first saw him, I didn't know that John could run. It's funny when I made the comment to Billy about us going to some Super Bowls. It was purely after watching him throw the ball. It was at some point later when I saw John do the Houdini act when people were rushing, and he could scramble to his right and get almost to the right sideline, and if you came open on the left side of the field 30 yards down field, he could make that pass. It was a revelation to us that we had a chance finally to play with someone whose skill level was such that we knew.

"Again, I knew that the guy I was watching throw was going to the Super Bowl. I just didn't know when. I was hoping it would happen when I was still on the team. I thank him for making it possible for me to go to another Super Bowl."

CHAPTER THREE

THE DRIVE

W hat helped make The Drive so unique was its series of fortunate mishaps, imperfections that became pieces to a 15-play sum of perfection. And it wasn't just the messed-up kickoff return everyone refers to. There was also a potentially momentum-stopping sack that brought up third and 18 near midfield followed by a snap off the butt of a receiver in motion. There were one or two other nuanced miscues that weren't noticeable until talking later to the principals involved. So perfectly imperfect was The Drive that catapulted John Elway's career with the first of his two signature moments. (If you don't know the second, harken back to late in the third quarter of Super Bowl XXXII.)

The Drive occurred in the final five minutes of the 1986 AFC Championship Game played in the extremely hostile setting of Cleveland's Municipal Stadium. The foe was the championship-starved Cleveland Browns, who had just taken a 20–13 lead thanks to a long touchdown pass from quarter-back Bernie Kosar to receiver Brian Brennan with less than six minutes remaining.

The Drive did start, as everyone knows, with the bungled kickoff return. It wasn't a muff, as it's often described, but an ill-advised decision by Ken Bell to pick up Mark Moseley's line-drive, bad-hop kickoff near the goal line. There was nothing Bell could do about the bad hop. The low kick wasn't catchable as it bounced too far in front of Bell. It's whether or not he should have picked up the bouncing sphere before it stopped bouncing that comes into question. Would the kick have reached the end zone for a touchback? We'll never know, thank goodness. It worked out better this way. "Go back to the play before The Drive. I'm on the kickoff return," said linebacker Tom Jackson, who was playing the second-to-last game of his Broncos Ring of Fame career. "The last thing we're talking about as we go on the field is we have to get a good return. We've got to give them some field position. The ball gets bobbled at the goal line. I run back and I never did turn around to block because there's no reason. The ball is not coming toward us. This mayhem is happening right at the goal line. That's all I can see as I'm running back. When I got to the ball and saw where it was, it was on the 1 ½-yard line. I always tell people there was a half a yard to the second yard. It was closer to 99 than it was 98."

During the initial meeting with Denver Broncos owner Pat Bowlen in his office during training camp of 2005, he made two points. Mr. B, as he was called, said that: one, Mike Shanahan, a longtime Broncos assistant offensive coach, was not ready to become a successful head coach until he spent three years with the San Francisco 49ers as an offensive coordinator from 1992 to 1994. The Bill Walsh Way in San Francisco led to two decades of dominance for the 49ers—and later a three-year run of greatness for the Broncos. And, two, it wasn't until Elway's fourth season that he was ready to execute The Drive.

The latter was more reminder than news but still it emphasized the point that seasoning is necessary before greatness blooms. Lining up under guard instead of center, throwing more interceptions (52) than touchdowns (47) yet still managing to post an impressive record (27–13), were part of Elway's initial three-year development. "Every NFL defensive player knows the way to get to a young quarterback, I don't care how good he is, is to blitz him," said Steve Foley, a starting safety who was in his 11th and final year with the Broncos in 1986. "And punish him and welcome him to the league. And there was no lack of that. They came after him. In some respects he was held back. Because he was young, I think Dan [Reeves] held him back, and he probably would have been better off letting him go a little more. But he was careful. He did not want John to get PTSD every time he went back to pass. So we still depended on our run game."

In year four Elway threw 19 touchdown passes against 13 interceptions and posted the best passer rating of his young career. His 79.0 rating may pale by today's standards, but in

1986 it ranked 11th among league passers. The best ranking that year was the 92.6 posted by Minnesota Vikings quarterback Tommy Kramer. In 2023 that 92.6 rating would have tied for 14th.

There was less dinking and dunking and more downfield throws among quarterbacks in 1986. And Elway set the standard. The flair and the downfield passes were both part of The Drive. "That '86 year when we went to the Super Bowl, I thought we had an awfully good team, and John was just coming on," Foley said. "The Drive culminated that. You just knew at that time he could get it done. To have a game like that on the road to win the AFC championship in a tough place, the Dawg Pound—that last pass he threw on a slant to Mark Jackson, that's his whole body he put into it, and he just drilled it. That was an unbelievable moment."

It was January 11, 1987, amid muddy, chilly conditions. With the score tied 13–13 and less than six minutes remaining in the fourth quarter, Kosar lofted a do-or-die ball down the left side of the chopped-up field to Brennan, who outmaneuvered an off-balance safety Dennis Smith to catch it. As Smith fell, Brennan waltzed into the end zone for a 48-yard touchdown. The sellout crowd of nearly 80,000 went berserk as the Browns went ahead by a touchdown with 5:43 remaining in regulation.

The stadium's noise then soared to inaudible levels as Moseley's kickoff lined short, then took a bad hop left, and bounded toward the goal line. Bell raced back to pick up the ball. NBC's color analyst Merlin Olsen made the remark that Bell should have let the ball bounce into the end zone for a touchback but panicked and picked it up instead. Upon securing the ball, Bell was immediately swarmed. It's hard to know whether the bouncing kickoff would have reached the end zone had Bell not picked it up. In hindsight, Bell had nothing to lose by letting it go, but, of course, that was easy for Olsen and everyone else to say. It's not so easy to make a split-second decision during pressure-packed live action with 79,973 bundled fans roaring in excited anticipation.

Thank goodness Bell picked the ball up. Otherwise, there would have been no touchdown march for the ages if, say, the ball was brought out to the 20 on a touchback.

There was a TV timeout with 5:32 remaining as the Broncos offense, sans Elway, huddled up in the end zone. Elway was on the sideline talking over the first few plays with Coach Reeves as left guard Keith Bishop from his huddle position defiantly uttered his famous line, "We got 'em right where we want 'em."

Only that was the cleaned-up version. "Isn't it always with Bish?" receiver Steve Watson said with a chuckle. "Bish was one of the guys who was like the glue in our whole group. He was our enforcer. There wasn't a moment on the field when you didn't realize he had your back. We played Cleveland once. That linebacker they had, Clay Matthews, one play I cracked back on him. I guess he thought it was a cheap shot. And he came after me, and Bishop came up and wiped him out."

Bishop set the record straight on his brief, motivational huddle speech. "We're down there and we're in the huddle, and I don't think John was in there," Bishop said in *The 50 Greatest Players in Denver Broncos History*. "He comes back in the huddle, and everyone is laughing their asses off and he's like, 'What? What?' So we're in the huddle, we're waiting, and we're looking at the Browns. And several of the Browns were good friends of mine. They're all standing in their defensive huddle and they're all laughing. And I said, '[Bleep] them [bleep, bleeps], we've got those [bleeps] right where we want them.'"

Not all of those words made it to folklore or the morning papers. "They left some words out of it," Bishop said. "And if we hadn't driven and scored, nobody would have heard anything about it."

From the end zone opposite the Dawg Pound, Elway, whose right shoulder of his jersey and right pant leg already were caked in mud from an earlier play, broke the huddle and on the first play threw a flare pass to running back Sammy Winder, who caught it for a five-yard gain. That created a little breathing room, as they say, for second and 5 at the 7-yard line. "Here's what I remember about The Drive: as a rookie I would get in on third down so Steve Watson is starting at the wing position," said Mark Jackson, a rookie receiver in 1986 who made the two biggest receptions on The Drive. "Vance Johnson was starting at the Y position. We went a lot of two-receiver sets except in two minutes. Our two-minute drill was mostly three wides, in which case I had an opportunity to get into the game."

A pitch right to Winder was smothered following a short gain to bring up third and 2 at the 10. Winder, the best 3.33 yards-per-carry back in Broncos history because of his ability to pick up just enough tough yards on short yardage and goal-line situations, needed a second effort to pick up the first down at the 12. It was close enough to where the officials had to bring out the sticks to measure. "You look back at The Drive," Reeves said at his Ring of Fame induction ceremony in 2014. "And Winder barely picks up the first down. If he doesn't get it, what do we do? Do we punt there?"

He shrugged. The measurement came with 4:11 left in regulation. Reeves didn't say what he would have done had Winder came up short, but his shrug indicated punting would have been a logical option. The idea would have been to have the Denver defense stop them and get the ball back with about two minutes remaining rather than put the entire game on fourth and 1 at the Broncos' own 11. The decision was moot, of course. Winder got just enough.

Winder had one more three-yard run on first down, which turned out to be the last time he was needed on this possession. Winder had the first four plays of The Drive, picking up 13 yards. Elway had the rest.

A second-down scramble for 11 yards by Elway, who dove forward across the first down line, put the ball at his own 26. Elway was just 1-for-1 for five yards at that point on the drive, but the Broncos had picked up two first downs while moving the ball out from their 1 ½-yard line to the 26. Elway's growing confidence was palpable. He heated up. A bullet over the middled to running back Steve Sewell, who came out of a split backfield to the right and jumped up and twisted back to catch the pass as he was getting hit by Browns safety Chris Rockins, picked up 22 yards. *Uh-oh, Browns fans.* The Broncos were out to their 48-yard line with a first down.

Nearly 37 years later, Elway reflected on Marty Schottenheimer's Cleveland defense. "They played pretty soft," he said. "There was a lot more room there than there was earlier in the game. And I could run a little bit, got outside a little bit. And Dan had to turn it loose, right?"

Elway smiled. Forever the talk about the 10-year, Reeves-Elway era was that Reeves played a conservative, Elway-stifling offense for three-and-a-half quarters and then let his quarterback do his thing to go win the game. The Drive would be the prototype.

On the final play before the two-minute warning, Elway fired a fastball to the right sideline where Watson made a 12-yard catch between two defenders. Elway went to the sideline to confer with Reeves as the Broncos were now up to the Browns' 40 with 1:59 remaining. "When John came to the sideline, it's almost easy to say afterward, but the look of determination and confidence and 'can't wait to get my hands on the ball' was all over him," Tom Jackson said. "It was the moment where we saw what he does. It was the moment that he revealed to us what he does, who he is. When an athlete of that caliber does that and you are fortunate enough to see it and be a part of it…there's a moment when people discovered Steph Curry is the greatest shooter ever. There's some moment in a game where everybody saw it, but his team saw it every day."

The plan discussed at the two-minute warning, though, immediately went haywire. Elway's first down pass from the Browns' 40 went deep incomplete as Johnson was well-covered. On second down Elway stepped up in the pocket to avoid an edge pass rush from Matthews, who was driven down by Bishop. But defensive tackle Dave Puzzuoli, who had initially been pancaked by center Billy Bryan on the play, got up off the ground and ran right into Elway for an eight-yard sack.

The Drive was in serious trouble. The Broncos had third and 18 at the Browns' 48 as the clock ticked inside 1:40. Further disaster was avoided when Bryan's shotgun snap glanced off the left hip of Watson, who was in motion from left to right. Watson was nicknamed "Blade" as a rookie by Broncos head coach Red Miller because of his slender frame. Never has a Broncos player ever possessed such a fortunate build. "Being as skinny as I was," Watson said, "that was a benefit in that case."

Elway nonchalantly bent down to nab the ricocheted snap, dropped back a few more steps, cocked, and hummed a fastball to Mark Jackson, who ran a deep-in route from the outside left position, caught it in the open, and turned for a 20-yard gain. First down.

The Drive was humming. "That third-and-18 play, I'm in the huddle, John had been sacked the play before that set us back, and I had a pretty good idea that play might be called," Mark Jackson said. "We had used that play several times throughout the season and we didn't have a lot of plays where you could pick up 18 yards in one chunk. I think Dan's mindset was usually we have two plays to pick this up. This was one play we ran to perfection throughout the year. It's a two-receiver slot play where Vance Johnson clears out on a skinny post or a 9 [go] route, and I come underneath him on a crossing route. The play runs pretty consistent depending on what the defense is. If you have man coverage, then the route is going to be different than zone coverage. In this particular case, they rolled up in a zone. They were just trying to protect the first-down marker, and I was able to bend the play back out and kind of nestled down in a little hole, and John fired a rocket in there."

The receiver said the play—huge as it was—could have been better. "I always told Vance, 'I think John was a little tired or something because he didn't clear out the safety like he should have,'" Mark Jackson said. "If he had, I would have had a touchdown because the cornerback fell down, and it was the safety that made the tackle. In the same breath, if he had cleared the safety out and I did score a touchdown, there would be no Drive, which is the same thing I tell Ken Bell, who was my roommate that year."

The clock ticked inside 1:30, but The Drive was alive with a first down at the Browns' 28. Elway threw his first-down pass away, stopping the clock with 1:19 remaining. The NBC cameras picked up backup quarterback Gary Kubiak on the sidelines discussing the next play call with Reeves. "Yeah, back in those days we didn't have the helmet stuff, so everything was signaled," Kubiak said. "I was the guy who signaled all the plays to John through Dan. Dan would call all the plays. Our preparation back in those days was so different. Nowadays they're able to tell you everything in their helmet. That changed the game in a lot of ways as far as how much information they can give the quarterback. Back then all you would get is the play. And then the quarterback had to set the formation, had to set the snap. You had to do a lot of work that you don't have to worry about now."

On second and 10, Elway flipped a screen left to Sewell, who was in the clear as he grabbed the ball and picked up 14 yards down the left side for a first down at the Browns' 14.

The screen to Sewell was arguably the best *call* of The Drive.

With the clock now inside a minute, Elway lofted a pass to the right end zone for Watson, who caught it but well out of bounds. It was second and 10 from the 14 with 49 seconds left. From the shotgun Elway quickly took off on what almost appeared to be a planned run. Elway ran right and dropped into a hook slide a yard short of the first down but out of bounds to stop the clock. Elway's uniform was caked in mud from pad to toe. Besides all of his bullet passes, Elway now had two runs for 20 yards on The Drive.

It was third and 1 from the Browns' 5-yard line with 42 seconds remaining. Next came the play that has been replayed and seen by Broncos fans hundreds of times over the past 40 years. Standing five yards back from center in the shotgun, Elway took the snap, dropped back another six yards, planted his feet the best he could in the chewed up, cloddy conditions, and hummed a fastball midway to the end zone. A falling Mark Jackson caught it in his gut, quickly bounced up, and levitated into a rising spike right in front of the Dawg Pound. Elway raised both arms in celebration and jogged toward the sidelines.

When Elway was asked 39 years later what he most remembered about The Drive, he mentioned the feeling he had as he threw the touchdown pass to Jackson. "When I threw the touchdown to Mark, I wanted to throw it outside because I was worried about going inside. I didn't want to go inside in case I didn't see someone coming over," Elway said. "The corner fell off on the shoe route [run out of the backfield by Gerald Willhite]. So they zoned it up and they took that shoe route away so Mark was open. But I remember thinking I'm going to throw this as hard as I can throw it because if Mark doesn't catch it, I don't want anybody else catching it. If you watch how hard I threw that ball, I did throw it as hard as I can throw it."

It's been said, including by Elway himself, that Elway put more mustard on that touchdown throw to Jackson than any other. That may not be the case because Elway's back foot slipped and twisted as he fired. "It was slippery, but I know my intention," Elway said. "And then you see it so many times and you look at, I think, it was [Carl] Hairston inside gets his hand up, and it just barely misses his hand."

The Drive has taken on a mythical life of its own and with how hard Elway threw that last pass. "I've heard him in different interviews say that," Mark Jackson said. "He understood as a quarterback he had two plays to score. He said he threw that ball as hard as he could...How many times have we seen—i.e., Russell Wilson in the Super Bowl—try to stick one in there and you throw a pick? So, yeah, he said that's the hardest he's ever thrown a ball. I'd probably have to agree with him."

The 5'9" Jackson had the most famous touchdown catch in Broncos' history (rivaled only perhaps 25 years later by Demaryius Thomas' catch, stiff-arm, and 80-yard run off a Tim Tebow pass that gave Denver a walk-off playoff win in the 2011 season). But, of course, Jackson's catch propelled the Broncos to a Super Bowl appearance. "In that particular case, being vertically challenged was a benefit," Jackson said. "I don't think Jerry Rice could have made that play. I just had to go down and dig it out of the dirt. My job on that play was to rub the linebacker to get him to run over the top, and usually John threw that ball out to the flat. I did the job, I made the linebacker run over the top, and I looked out to the flat, I gave a quick glimpse over my shoulder, and I noticed the ball wasn't there, and as I looked back into pocket, I see John

Elway's eyes are about the size of saucers. And he's got that arm cocked back. I'm like, *Oh my God, he had never thrown me the ball ever on that play.* On the other [third-and-18] play, I always got the ball. About 80 percent of the time, he threw the ball to me. So it was a totally different reaction and mindset as I was going through that play."

The extra-point kick by barefooted kicker Rich Karlis tied it 20–20 with 39 seconds remaining. Karlis then nearly made a huge mistake by booting his kickoff out of bounds. But instead of giving the receiving team the ball at 40, as is the case today, the penalty then was five yards back and re-kick. Karlis then drilled a one-hopper down the middle, the Browns struggled to handle it, and after a safe screen pass, Schottenheimer had his team kneel away the final 16 seconds to settle for overtime.

In overtime the Broncos called heads, but it was tails, and the Browns took the ball. They had third and 2 at their own 37, but Schottenheimer—to his forever postseason demise—played it safe, and a run play was stuffed. The Broncos got their first overtime possession at their own 25. It's all they would need. "The thing about The Drive is we still had to go do it in overtime," Elway said for perhaps the 390th time in his life.

On second and 5, Elway drilled a 22-yard completion to rookie tight end Orson Mobley, who made a nice, half-diving catch. The Broncos were in business with a first down on the Browns' 48. Not for long. A pitch to Winder lost two yards, and a screen pass fell incomplete.

On third and 12, Elway made as big a play as he had all game, even counting any play he made during The Drive. Backpedaling straight back to his own 37, Elway broke the pocket and scrambled left as Sam Clancy was pass rushing to Elway's right. Near the left sideline, Elway threw on the run, threw off his off foot, and fired a 28-yard completion to Watson near the sideline.

The Broncos then had the ball at the Browns' 22. Elway had done it again. Three Winder runs moved the ball to the 15. With the ball smack dab in the middle of the field, Karlis slightly hooked his 33-yard field goal attempt with the ball traveling inside the left goal post by a fraction. But it was still good, and the Broncos won 23–20.

Elway had back-to-back drives to lead the Broncos to their second of five Super Bowls. And the 98-and-a-half-yard march in the final five-plus minutes of regulation went down in lore as The Drive. "Man, I'm starting to know every play of that Drive," Mark Jackson said. "In fact, it's part of my presentation when I speak."

Narrating "The Drive" for the NFL Network, comedian Steve Harvey, who grew up in Cleveland a die-hard Browns' fan, said after The Drive was finished, "You could have heard a rat pissing on a ball of cotton in a corner in my dude's basement. We was crushed, man, completely crushed."

Mark Jackson said he still uses Harvey's line in his presentations. Meanwhile, Watson still relishes it. "That was fun," Watson said. "Just going down the field, we knew that even with all the quirky things that happened in that Drive, you felt like, *Okay, we can do this.* The crowd was irrelevant. They didn't play into the picture. When he got in the huddle, it was 100 percent absolute confidence. We knew. He looked at us, we looked at him, and we just knew we were going to get it done."

Kubiak had the best seat in the house, standing next to Coach Reeves on the sidelines to relay the plays to his buddy Elway. After his plays were sent in, Kubiak marveled at Elway's performance—both executing the play that was delivered and improvising when the play went off script. "That was the start of something special," Kubiak said. "We had a playoff team our rookie year, and Dan started Steve DeBerg in a playoff game. We were a playoff team or close to it the first three years, but to go on the road in the NFL, to go to Cleveland, which was an extremely successful organization and team, and to walk in there with that weather and that stadium, that environment, and for him to take our team down the field 98 yards, or whatever it was, in that environment left you with: I know one thing we'll have a chance to win every week as long as this guy plays. There's not many guys who can do that. So I would say that was a big, big part of what was to come."

The only problem with The Drive was the encore became anticlimactic. It led to the first of three consecutive Super Bowl blowouts for the Broncos. And losing big in Super Bowls led to irreconcilable differences between Elway and his head coach. "I didn't think anybody could beat us after The Drive to beat the Browns," Foley said. "I thought we could handle the Giants. We played them late in the season and we were subbing in guys, and they didn't have a super offense. Now Phil Simms had the game of his life, and I thought Bill Parcells coached an incredible game where he went away from his usual game plan. Anyway, John was just getting started. And that game was maybe the best he ever played."

CHAPTER FOUR

THE ELWAY-REEVES ERA

T he not-so-secret friction between the young quarterback John Elway and his domineering head coach Dan Reeves began with the most rudimentary of reasons: the way plays were called. To Elway, Reeves' play-calling system was ass backward. "Dan was here 10 years, and it was an odd to the right, even to the left numbering system," Elway said. "And I never got it."

The West Coast system Elway ran at Stanford—or any offensive system he operated from youth football on through Granada Hills High School and Stanford—used a numbering system where even numbers were used for plays or players to the right, odd numbers for plays and players to the left. A *33 Dive* is a handoff to the fullback at the hole or gap between the left guard and left tackle. A *26 Toss* is a pitch right to the halfback or tailback. It's Football 101, a universal numbering system.

Think about it. When you've brushed your teeth with your right hand every day of your life, there is something locked in the brain that won't ever let a person brush his teeth with his left hand without total concentration. Reeves' numbering system went counter to the universe.

"Every time it was odd numbering system, I had to go, 'to the right, to the right, to the right' because you've done it your whole life where it's even to your right, odd to the left," Elway said. "So it's automatic. I could never get that switched so everything was backward. I heard Dan switched later. I don't know. But everyone else was even right, odd on left. Everybody else had to change. It was so unnatural. I always had to think about it instead of reacting to it because it was so backward."

Joe Lombardi was the Denver Broncos' offensive coordinator for first-year head coach Sean Payton in 2023. That's one thing he is known for. Another is that he is one of the grandchildren of Vince Lombardi, arguably the best head coach in NFL history. (To which Green Bay Packers fans would say, where's the argument?) Elway's water-drip torture with odd to the right, even to the left was relayed to Joe Lombardi, who immediately chuckled in recognition. "It's funny you say that," Lombardi said.

Lombardi relayed how he stumbled across one of his grandfather's old play sheets. He quickly detected something odd about it. Or something to the right about it. "The numbering system had odd numbers to the right and even numbers to the left," Lombardi said. "Everyone else has even numbers to the right, odd to the left. I had heard the only two coaches who did it the other way was my grandfather

56

and Tom Landry. They were both coaches for the New York Giants, and I guess their coach wanted them to do it different from the other teams."

The so-called Greatest Game Ever Played was the 1958 NFL Championship Game in which the Baltimore Colts' Johnny Unitas came up with his own impressive drive to beat the New York Giants 23–17 in sudden death overtime. One of the more common trivia pieces from that game was the assistant coaches from the losing team. History now shows Giants head coach Jim Lee Howell had the greatest coordinator duo in NFL history in Vince Lombardi as offensive coordinator and Tom Landry as his defensive coordinator. (And the fact Unitas beat them demonstrates how great he was.)

Vince Lombardi went on to become head coach of the Packers, immediately transforming the 1–10–1 team he inherited to 7–5–2 in his first year of 1959 to the NFL Championship Game in his second year of 1960 to winning five NFL titles, including Super Bowl I and II, in his next seven seasons from 1961 to 1967.

Lombardi's greatest rival at the end of his Packers' coaching term was Landry's Dallas Cowboys. Landry took a bit longer to bring championships to Dallas. For starters, the Cowboys were the first of the modern-era expansion franchises when the NFL awarded Dallas a team in 1960. There was a catch—the Cowboys couldn't participate in the 1960

NFL Draft. *Thanks, NFL.* Landry's Cowboys went 0–11–1 in their first season.

Improvement was gradual until 1965 when the Cowboys drafted the likes of quarterback Craig Morton in the first round, defensive tackle Jethro Pugh in the 11th round, running back Merv Rettenmund (who played for the baseball Baltimore Orioles instead) in the 19th, and signed South Carolina's all-time leading passer in Reeves as an undrafted college free agent with the idea of converting him to safety.

When the Cowboys suffered several injuries to their halfback position in 1965, Reeves was moved over to the offensive side of the ball. The Cowboys went 7–7 that year for their first non-losing season. Reeves' first full season at halfback in 1966 was his second year as a pro. He rushed for 757 yards and eight touchdowns and caught 41 passes for another 557 yards and eight touchdowns. All in a 14-game season. He was like the Christian McCaffrey of yesteryear.

The Cowboys went 10–3–1 during the regular season, then lost to Lombardi's Packers in the NFL Championship Game when Tom Brown intercepted Don Meredith in the end zone with less than a minute to play. The Cowboys again met the Packers in the championship the next year, but this time it was in Green Bay for what became the famed Ice Bowl. Reeves threw a halfback pass to Lance Rentzel for a 50-yard touchdown in the fourth quarter to give the Cowboys a 17–14 lead. Anyone reading this book is enough of a football historian to know how that game ended. Bart Starr ran a fourth-down, quarterback sneak behind a Jerry Kramer block on Pugh for a one-yard touchdown with 13 seconds remaining, and Lombardi beat Landry again.

Reeves tore knee ligaments early in 1968 season and when it became obvious during his 1969 comeback he wasn't the same player he became Landry's protégé as player/coach from 1970 to 1972 before becoming a full-time Cowboys assistant coach. From 1978 to 1980, Reeves was the Cowboys' offensive coordinator and in Dallas he had even numbered plays to the left, odd numbered plays to the right.

In 1981 he became the youngest head coach in the NFL when he was hired by Broncos owner Edgar Kaiser Jr. Two years later, Kaiser swung a trade for the quarterback phenom that was John Elway. A year after that in March 1984, Kaiser sold the Broncos to Pat Bowlen, leaving the new owner to inherit his coach, Reeves, and quarterback, Elway.

* * *

Let the record show that by 2014, 22 years after Dan Reeves had been fired as Denver Broncos head coach, time had healed old wounds, and John Elway does not hold a grudge. "He certainly doesn't," said a chuckling Dan Reeves, fresh off a golf outing as he learned he had been elected into the Broncos Ring of Fame. "When you look at it, John was a big part of my coaching career. We won 100 games. I have a great deal of respect for him as a player and what he's accomplished."

Tension, though, filled the relationship of Reeves, the head coach, and Elway, the superstar quarterback for the better part of 10 seasons. It never really got in the way of their ability to do business. Reeves, who passed away New Year's Day 2022 just shy of his 78th birthday, still coached the Broncos to victory more times than not, and Elway became irrefutably one of the game's biggest superstars.

But there was tension. Even at times a strong dislike for each other.

As a young quarterback, Elway sometimes felt stifled by Reeves' conservative approach. They won together; Reeves would turn Elway loose for numerous fourth-quarter comebacks, and they reached the Super Bowl following the 1986, 1987, and 1989 seasons. "That's the thing. The one thing Dan did is he won everywhere he went," Elway said in mid-November 2023. "There was a method to his madness. The players he drafted always fit his style, and he got a lot out of them."

That doesn't mean they didn't clash along the way. "Yeah, you look back, we're all stubborn," Elway admitted.

Karl Mecklenburg, the Broncos' best defensive player during the decade-long, Reeves-Elway era, concurred. "They were the same. They were so similar that it made it difficult for them to get along. Both of them wanted to win so bad. If I could boil Dan down to one thing, it was: I have to win. That was Dan. And John was the same way. They each were stubborn, and each thought they knew how that was supposed to work. John wanted the ball in his hands when it was game time. But we were three-yards-and-a-cloud-of-dust, the old Tom Landry, until it was two minutes and John was calling the plays at the line of scrimmage and doing his thing."

Conservative, yes. Exasperating, no doubt. But the formula worked. "I'll say this: because we were that type of offense, we were better defensively," Mecklenburg said. "We were better as a team, I think. That was the way football was played in that era. The people that were winning championships were not the run-and-shoot guys and the throw the ball all over the field. It wasn't the Dan Marinos or the Warren Moons. That's not how it was done."

There may have been a time when Elway was a tad envious of Marino. They came in together in the 1983 NFL Draft. Elway was the first of six quarterbacks taken in the first round; Marino was the last of six. Yet, it was Marino with coach Don Shula who was able to set all the single-season and career passing records.

But while Marino was the better pure passer, Elway was the more prolific winner. With five Super Bowl appearances and two world championships, he had won more than any other modern-era quarterback at the time of his retirement. Marino reached the Super Bowl just one time and was wiped out in his lone Big Game by Joe Montana's San Francisco 49ers. Elway was 2–3 in Super Bowls, with his two wins coming in the final two years of his playing career when Mike Shanahan, not Reeves, was his head coach. "Would you like to have more numbers or whatever? Sure," Elway said. "Marino has all the numbers, but he only went to that one Super Bowl early."

Counting playoffs Elway was 96–57–1 in his 10 seasons with Reeves as head coach. He earned an NFL MVP award in 1987, so he wasn't completely restricted individually. There were three AFC championships. That's a lot of success for a head coach and quarterback who couldn't get along. "I look at it this way: in all my years in the NFL playing and coaching, if you have the…coaches and quarterbacks, it's never perfect in those environments," said Gary Kubiak, who had the unique perspective as Elway's backup quarterback for nine years and offensive coordinator for four. "You're battling each other every day, you're trying to win, you're trying to do the right thing, you're both under a lot of scrutiny. I mean, some of that is part of the job. Dan was a helluva football coach.

John was one of the greatest players to ever play the game. During their time we won a lot of football games. They just didn't get the Big One. You look back and go back-to-back years and you go to three Super Bowls in four years...But the end result is what everybody looks at, and that's what made it tough."

Did Reeves limit Elway's enormous abilities a little too much? Most of Elway's former teammates say he did. But then again... "Dan Reeves, it was hard to argue with the success that he had," said receiver Mark Jackson. "We went to three Super Bowls in four years. But he's going to be criticized because he had a very conservative approach. But I don't know. It's hard to tell what would have worked better. I think what hurt us in those Super Bowls was the fact we were in full pads the Wednesday and Thursday before the Super Bowl. It was old-school NFL. I think Walsh from San Francisco was the first one who by midseason said, 'We don't need to beat each other up anymore. I think you know how to tackle, I think you know how to play football. Let's take off the pads and put on shells and preserve the body.' I think that was a big issue."

When Reeves was fired after the 1992 season, he immediately was hired by the New York Giants to become their head coach in 1993. He brought former Broncos: Jackson, linebacker Michael Brooks, kicker Brad Daluiso, and punter Mike Horan with him to New York.

Elway wasn't going anywhere as owner Pat Bowlen used head coach Wade Phillips and offensive coordinator Jim Fassel as a two-year transition between Reeves and Shanahan. "They were opening it up with Jim Fassel," Jackson said. "I was so jealous. I wanted to be back in Denver so bad. You look at the numbers in '93. John had the most pass attempts in his career, most completions in his career, he had the most yards in his career. Only time he went over 4,000. But they were 9–7. So it didn't necessarily translate to championships."

Jackson's memory was accurate. In 1993, the year after Reeves was fired and replaced by Phillips and Fassel, Elway completed a career-best 63.2 percent of his passes on a career-most 348 completions off 551 attempts. He threw for 4,030 yards, which held up as his single-season best. He threw for 25 touchdowns against just 10 interceptions for a 92.8 passer rating that held as his best until his final season of 1998, when he posted a 93.0 rating.

Yet, Elway and the Broncos missed the playoffs with their 9–7 record. Meanwhile, that same year Reeves, the first-year Giants coach, transformed the 6–10 team he inherited from Ray Handley and guided them to an 11–5 record and a first-round playoff win. Although that success shows Reeves' coaching merits, the feeling was that Reeves could have found a happier medium. A medium that made Elway happier and still won. Maybe even the Big One.

Instead Reeves kept his star quarterback on a leash. "I don't know if anybody knows the reason," Tom Jackson said. "I don't know the reason. I don't know why he wasn't as trusting as obviously he should have been. I mean it was pretty obvious John was what he was, and it didn't seem like that was taken full advantage of. That's all. I know Dan Reeves wanted to win as many games as he could. That's obvious. But you want the quarterback to excel as much as he can in whatever ways you can help him. The Super Bowl that they finally win, I had the good fortune to be on the sideline because Pat [Bowlen] made sure I could be if I wanted. I asked for a sideline pass, and Pat got me—I'll never forget it—a go-anywhere-you-want pass. Watching them take apart the Green Bay Packers and getting a chance to see it up close was as gratifying as anything I experienced in my own career, almost felt better than playing football just because of the nature of what it was. All of us with the Denver Broncos, who had lost Super Bowls in the past, and here was John and company finally taking care of business against the defending world champions...I get chills even now thinking about it. It's one of those things I'll never forget."

Another memorable win, of course, happened in the AFC Championship Game, which featured The Drive. That was when Elway figured it out. He finished 22-of-38 for 244 yards but was a combined 8-of-12 for 128 yards in his drive to end regulation and one overtime possession that resulted in Rich Karlis' game-winning field goal. Those two drives are when Elway became Elway. "It might have been more Reeves figuring it out," wide receiver Steve Watson said. "It was that, 'Hey, this is probably what we should do.' There were times I would be downfield running all over the place, and John would throw it the length of the field, and we'd score just because there was no way anyone else was getting to it."

The Drive was a prelude to the Broncos' second ever Super Bowl appearance and the first of five for Elway. But while the oddsmakers were no doubt impressed by how Elway operated his 98 ½-yard drive for a game-tying touchdown in the AFC Championship Game against the Cleveland Browns, they didn't give him or his team much chance against the Giants, who in 1986 were led by gruff head coach Bill Parcells. The 1986 season was the year of Lawrence Taylor. The Giants outside linebacker revolutionized the way NFL defenses played. The edge rusher recorded an astounding 20.5 sacks.

This was the year after the Chicago Bears blitzed through the league with their famed 46 defense that pitched back-to-back shutouts in the NFC playoffs and became widely considered the best, and most feared, defense of all time. Giants defensive coordinator Bill Belichick answered the next year with Taylor, who became only the second defensive player in NFL history to be named MVP and first since Minnesota Vikings' defensive tackle Alan Page in 1971. To this day, Page and Taylor are the only defensive players who have won the league's overall MVP award.

Because of Taylor and the dominant Giants defense that also included Carl Banks, Leonard Marshall, Pepper Johnson, and Harry Carson, the Broncos were established as a sizeable nine-and-a-half point underdog for Super Bowl XXI. The Giants didn't need a drive from their ball-controlled, Phil Simms-engineered offense to get there. After going 14–2 in the regular season and earning a first-round bye, the Giants pulverized Montana's 49ers 49–3 in a second-round playoff game and shut out the Washington Redskins 17–0 in the NFC Championship Game. Three points in two NFC playoff games put the Giants in company with the '85 Bears, who had allowed zero points in two NFC playoff games.

One of the greater injustices of Elway's career was the perception he played poorly in his first three Super Bowls. That's not true in the case of his first Super Bowl appearance against the Giants. At halftime of Super Bowl XXI, Elway was 13-of-20 for 187 yards. He had completions of 54 yards to Vance Johnson, 31 to Watson, and 24 to Mark Jackson. He ran for a touchdown to put the Broncos up 10–7 after the first quarter and he engineered a drive to the Giants' 1-yard line for a first and goal early in the second quarter. But the Giants' defense stuffed the Broncos, and Rich Karlis missed a chip-shot 23-yard field goal. Near the end of the first half, Elway again moved his team to the Giants' 16-yard line, but Karlis missed another short field goal—this one from 34 yards—just 18 seconds from intermission. The Broncos were up 10–9 at halftime, but they should have been up 16–9.

In the second half, Karlis' misses seemed to unravel the Broncos. Simms was 10-of-10 in the second half for 168 yards and two touchdowns as his team exploded to a 39–13 lead. Elway threw a 47-yard, consolation touchdown pass to Johnson late in the fourth quarter to bring the final score to 39–20. For the game Elway completed 22-of-37 for 304 yards with a touchdown and rushed for 27 yards, including a touchdown. He played quite well. It was an impressive effort in defeat. But because the Broncos would get humiliated in the following year's Super Bowl—going up 10–0 on the Redskins before getting steamrolled for 35 points in the second quarter of a 42–10 loss in XXII and then two years later by the Montana's 49ers by the score of 55–10 in Super Bowl XXIV—it was convenient to envelop Elway's performance against the Giants into his struggles against Washington and San Francisco and say he couldn't win the Big One.

Funny thing is: Elway played better in his first Super Bowl against the Giants (304 yards, 83.6 rating) to cap the 1986 season than he did when he won his first Super Bowl against the Green Bay Packers (123 yards, 51.9 rating) 12 years later. But his heroic scramble that culminated in the helicopter coupled with a run-smashing effort by Terrell Davis in an upset victory, and Bowlen proclaiming, "This One's for John!" enabled Elway to go down in lore as one of the NFL's greatest champions.

The Super Bowls against Washington and the 49ers were bad, as Elway seemed to be anchored with horrific defenses. Statistically, those two Super Bowls were his worst among the 22 postseason games he played. He completed just 10-of-26 for 108 yards with no touchdowns and two interceptions against the 49ers for a 19.4 passer rating that was the worst in any game since his rookie season of 1983.

The game against Washington couldn't have started better. On the Broncos' first offensive play, Elway threw a 56-yard touchdown pass to Ricky Nattiel. His second drive had a 32-yard completion to Mark Jackson and a 23-yard reception off a halfback pass by Steve Sewell, but the series stalled inside the 10, and the Broncos settled for a short Karlis field goal and a 10–0 lead. It was disaster from there. Elway, who was 3-of-4 for 94 yards and a touchdown on the first two series, finished 11-of-34 for 163 yards and three interceptions.

The shame was Elway had his two best playoff performances in the 1987 and 1989 AFC Championship Games to get the Broncos there. In his third consecutive defeat of the Browns in the AFC title game—after The Drive and the Earnest Byner "Fumble"—Elway threw for 385 yards and three touchdowns with no interceptions to post a 120.7 rating in a relatively easy 37–21 Broncos win.

Alas, Elway's great performances in the AFC Championship Games only led to Super Bowl humiliation. Nine years later Elway won his fourth AFC Championship Game at Pittsburgh, and his own mother asked her son, "Do we have to go?" All those embarrassments on the national stage were too much to bear.

"We were never competitive in any Super Bowls, but we won some AFC championships," said Shanahan, who was a top offensive assistant coach for Reeves from 1984 to 1987 and again from 1989 to 1991. "When I went back and looked at it, the NFC was physical. And John could make plays. Even back then when we went to three Super Bowls in four years, I was asked to talk at many clinics and those type of things. At that time I couldn't really put together good clinic tapes together because really it was just John making plays. You couldn't explain what he did. But when you look at us winning three AFC championships in four years, I sometimes would ask, 'Man, how did we do it?' And then each year, you take a look. It was John making plays when everything broke down."

Elway was becoming increasingly fed up with Reeves' offensive game planning and seemingly not following it with his play calling on gamedays. Elway let his head coach have it during a closed-door, clear-the-air, man-to-man meeting about 10 weeks into a miserable 1990 season, in which the team's 5–11 record was the only losing record the two had posted in their 10 years together.

Actually, it was not quite a one-on-one meeting. Shanahan, who was back with the Broncos as a top offensive assistant after "my sabbatical with the Raiders" as he put it years later, had grown weary of playing middle man in the Elway-Reeves feud. Reeves complained to Shanahan about Elway, and Elway complained to Shanahan about Reeves. Finally, Shanahan arranged for the Elway-Reeves meeting and sat quiet as a witness. Elway let loose on his coach, basically accusing Reeves of not going through with the game plan on gameday—not to mention going behind his back in trying to trade him. The insults got personal on both sides, but Elway was the one who opened with salvos. "We walked out of there, and John asked me what I thought," Shanahan said. "I said, 'Well it was good. I think you got me fired, but it was good to clear the air.'"

Told over breakfast in November 2023 of Shanahan's reaction, Elway laughed. Ugly as that clear-the-air meeting was in 1990, the Reeves-Elway relationship had not yet hit rock bottom. The happened the following offseason—a week or so prior to 1991 training camp.

Elway was playing at a card table in Lake Tahoe where he was told he had nearly been traded to Washington. "I was up at that Tahoe [celebrity golf] tournament sitting with Earnest Byner," Elway said of the running back. "We were playing blackjack. We sat down, and he was like, 'Damn, I thought we had you.' I said, 'What are you talking about?' He said, 'You didn't know what was going on?' I said, 'No.' He said, 'You were getting traded to us.' I don't know who else was involved, but I guess Pat [Bowlen] was the one who said no. Dan was going to trade me to Washington, which at the time would have been fine. They ended up winning the Super Bowl that year with Rypien."

Elway's mind was still whirring as he paused to take a bite of his breakfast. He used his napkin, then smiled. "So that was kind of the end of the relationship," Elway said.

Reeves would fire Shanahan as offensive coordinator, though not until after the 1991 season when the Broncos won the AFC West with a 12–4 record that secured a first-round playoff bye. The Broncos would advance to one more AFC Championship Game under Reeves thanks to one more heroic, last-minute, snatch victory-from-defeat march by Elway. In a second-round, divisional playoff game at old Mile High Stadium, the Broncos rallied from a 24–16, fourth-quarter deficit—a two-score game as the NFL was still three years away from adopting the two-point conversion—to defeat Warren Moon and the Houston Oilers 26–24 in what became known as Drive II. Actually, Elway came through with back-to-back, 12-play, scoring drives of 80-plus yards to finish the game.

The final series was eerily similar to The Drive in that it traveled 98 yards and it also deserved its own nickname: Drive II. "Drive II was harder because we didn't have any timeouts, and we had to convert two fourth downs," Elway said nearly 30 years later. "The Drive we had three timeouts. Then again, we had to score a touchdown to tie in Cleveland and against Houston we needed a field goal to win it. Similar in that we had to go 98 yards, and it was the final drive, but other than that the circumstances were different."

A great punt by Houston's Greg Montgomery was downed at the Broncos' 2-yard line with 2:07 remaining and the Broncos down 24–23. On the first play from his end zone, Elway hit Michael Young for 22 yards. Out of the hole, the Broncos then had a first down at the 24. But it got dicey after the two-minute warning. Two incompletions and a short pass to Nattiel set up fourth and 6 at the 28. Elway scrambled and broke out of a sack, moving to his left. He had enough speed to make it to the left sideline for a seven-yard run that was just enough for the first down and took him out of bounds to stop the clock with 1:17 remaining.

Then three straight incompletions brought up fourth and 10 at the 35 with 59 seconds remaining. Again, Elway high-stepped out of the pocket, moved left, and floated a pass near the left sideline to a wide-open Johnson, who reached back for the pass, turned, and scooted up the sideline for 44 yards. That gave Denver a first down at the Houston 21 with 50 seconds left. Already in field goal range, the Broncos ran Steve Sewell on a sweep right primarily to chew up some clock, but instead he gained 10 yards for another first down. With 20 seconds left and his job done, Elway went to the sideline to receive congratulations for a job well done as David Treadwell went out for a gimme, 28-yard field goal. Not so easy. The long snap was grounded back to Kubiak, the holder who deftly picked up the ball, set it down upright, and Treadwell knocked it through. "There are times when you know the situation is hopeless, and one look at John and we knew we had a chance," Young said. "That's got to be one of the greatest comebacks."

The following week the Broncos lost 10–7 in the AFC Championship Game to the Buffalo Bills. Elway threw a costly pick-six and was knocked out of the game with an injury prior to the fourth quarter. Kubiak played extremely well in relief, but it was the Bills—not the Broncos—who would go on to get creamed in the Super Bowl.

Ever audacious as boss of the Broncos, Reeves first fired Shanahan and essentially replaced him with Raymond Berry—the Hall of Fame receiver for the Baltimore Colts who was head coach of the New England Patriots team that played the foil to the great '85 Bears in Super Bowl XX—after the Buffalo loss. Reeves then made the controversial decision to draft UCLA sophomore quarterback Tommy Maddox with the No. 25 overall selection in the first round—and not wide receiver Carl Pickens, who went No. 31 to the Cincinnati Bengals in the 1992 draft. *Huh?* Elway was 31 years old, about to turn 32. Hardly over the hill. Pickens would have helped Elway here and now. Maddox was obviously expected to replace Elway in a year or two. "Dan was sticking it to me," Elway said. "I was at Stapleton waiting on my bag, and a guy came up and said, 'What'd you think about who you drafted today?' I asked him who we drafted. 'Tommy Maddox.' 'Ooohhh.' I didn't really get that mad because I thought Pickens must have been gone."

Nope. Elway learned later Pickens was still on the board when the Broncos selected.

When Elway battled injuries in 1992 and the Broncos went 0–4 in Maddox's four starts, Bowlen decided he had enough of the friction between Reeves and Elway. The Broncos' lousy performance with Maddox convinced Bowlen that it was his favorite quarterback—and not his head coach—that was the difference. After a 7–3 start that season, the Broncos swooned, losing five of their last six to miss the postseason with an 8–8 record. Someone had to go, and it wasn't going to be Elway. Reeves was fired. And while Reeves would again lead two more teams—the Giants and Atlanta Falcons—to successful seasons that included postseason berths and one more Super Bowl appearance, he never did win it all. It was Elway who wound up winning the Super Bowl without him. Twice.

Still, it took some patience. Elway wouldn't win the ultimate game until Shanahan took charge of not only the team as head coach, but also the Broncos' entire football operations. And Shanahan again took a couple years' detour to another organization before he returned to the Broncos for a third time. That organization was the 49ers, whose principles of Bill Walsh gave birth to an 18-year run of dominance. And thanks to his apprenticeship with the 49ers, Shanahan arrived back with the Broncos just in time.

The last time for Elway was a Super Bowl win against his former coach and one-time tormenter, Reeves. "When I go back, I appreciate both of them and their contributions to the game," Kubiak said. "Obviously John's contribution as a player, as a front-office guy, and what John contributed to the National Football League, it's really easy to say it's probably unmatched. So I have respect for all of them. I look back on those times and say it was part of football, and we battled and we were all trying to be the best we could be."

In their own way, Elway and Reeves were immensely successful—together and on their own. Reeves won 110 games and five division titles and three conference championships during his 12 years as Broncos coach (the first two without Elway). He later coached the Falcons to the 1998 season Super Bowl where he lost to the Broncos in Elway's final game as a player.

Elway later became a 10-year Broncos general manager and head of football operations. During that term he guided his franchise to five consecutive AFC West Division titles, two Super Bowl appearances, and one Super Bowl championship in his first five seasons.

Nearly two decades later, when Elway was in charge of Broncos football operations as the team's general manager, he didn't stop the team's Ring of Fame committee from electing Reeves in 2014. "He should be there," Elway said. "He went to three Super Bowls." After all, Reeves was the second best coach in Broncos history. How could he not be inducted among the team's greats? "I have great deal of appreciation for what Dan helped us achieve," Elway said while endorsing Reeves for the Ring of Fame. "He's a great football coach and is very deserving of this honor."

CHAPTER FIVE

THE SON
OF BUM ERA

There was a time before 9/11 and COVID-19 when the world was less fearful, the rules less restrictive. The NFL started taking over the world of American sports in 1994 through its exploding television revenues. One of the most memorable moments was a *Monday Night Football* game on October 17, 1994, at Denver's old Mile High Stadium, where the visiting Kansas City Chiefs took on the Denver Broncos.

It was memorable because it was a time when at the two-minute warning the NFL allowed the media to walk on the field outside the end zones to watch the rest of the game live at field level—not in the far upper reaches of a sterile, glassed-in press box. In this particular game, two of the most iconic quarterbacks in NFL history went at it—two-minute drive to two-minute drive. This was a matchup of two of the best of all time: 34-year-old Broncos quarterback John Elway vs. Chiefs 38-year-old quarterback Joe Montana.

The Chiefs were up 24–21 in a back-and-forth game that was thrilling but not necessarily well-played. With 2:45 remaining and Elway moving his Broncos to midfield, an inexplicable exchange of fumbles occurred. Broncos tight end

Shannon Sharpe fumbled the ball away after a seven-yard reception. And on the very next play, Chiefs running back Marcus Allen fumbled it right back to the Broncos. Two future Hall of Famers fumbled four seconds apart.

Elway and the Broncos had the ball at the Chiefs' 39, which was a mixed gift. Great field position, yes, but there simply was not enough real estate to chew up the remaining 2:41. This author was standing outside the south end zone and could see clearly Cedric Tillman step outside the end zone and then step back in to catch a four-yard touchdown pass from Elway. Can't do that. Incomplete. It was now third and goal from 4. On a designed run, Elway rumbled into the end zone for a touchdown.

Even though the Broncos were only 1–4 entering this game and the Chiefs were 3–2, the sold-out crowd of more than 75,000 and the participants on both sides created a playoff-like energy. Games played on Monday night can do that. Elway slammed the ball to the turf in celebration, raised his arms triumphantly, and screamed his joy at the standing, cheering, roaring fans in the south stands. The Broncos were up 28–24 with 1:29 remaining. "The man seems like he comes alive when he gets down to two minutes," Chiefs defensive end Neil Smith, who had three and a half of Kansas City's six sacks on Elway in the game, said in the postgame locker room. "You just know he's going to get it done."

The problem was there were still 89 seconds remaining. Wade Phillips, the beleaguered Broncos head coach of a team that started 0–4 amid high expectations, had just replaced beleaguered defensive coordinator Charlie Waters in calling the defensive plays. The incredibly soft defensive strategy was no match for Montana, who despite showing signs of physical wear and tear in what would be the final season of his 15-year career, was still cool and collected under pressure. Montana sliced and diced the Broncos' defense for seven completions in eight attempts, culminating the drive with a five-yard touch-down pass to Willie Davis for the game-winner with eight seconds remaining.

The Broncos lost 31–28 to fall to 1–5. "I've never been so tired in my life," Broncos star safety Dennis Smith said afterward. "This was the most exhausting game I've ever played in."

In his eighth try, head coach Marty Schottenheimer had his first win at Mile High. Montana, who was written off as washed up in *The Kansas City Star* Sunday sports column the day prior to the game, had his first Mile High win in four tries. "He's not that old is he?" Montana's wife, Jennifer, shouted up to the crowd as she walked in to join the media in the visiting team's press conferences.

"I didn't think we could have had any tougher losses than we had in the first four games, but this was tougher," Phillips said.

The day before, the San Francisco 49ers—with third-year offensive coordinator Mike Shanahan calling the plays—destroyed the Atlanta Falcons 42–3 to move to 5–2. Shanahan and the 49ers were on their way to leading the league in scoring for a third consecutive season and winning Super Bowl XXIX. From the *Monday Night Football* loss to the Chiefs on, Phillips and his coaching staff were on borrowed time.

NFL placekickers often don't emerge until a year or two after they turn pro and after they went undrafted. Adam Vinatieri, Justin Tucker, Matt Prater, and Brandon McManus are just some of the undrafted kickers who found great-to-decent success. So it was unusual when in the 1993 draft the Denver Broncos took Jason Elam, a kicker from Hawaii, with the second of their two third-round picks.

A renaissance man who piloted his own plane, authored novels, and visited far reaches of the world through his missionary work for Christian groups, Elam is more intelligent than the average person. He looks back on his years with the Broncos with a perspective worth hearing. His impressions of the Wade Phillips years? "I was a rookie so I didn't have any context coming in," Elam said 30 years after he was drafted. "But you could tell when I got there that everything hinged on John. He's in his prime, and we've got a chance to do something very cool. They had had some [postseason] runs and hadn't quite gotten there. I know that Coach Fassel and Wade, they were really excited. I thought we had a lot of weapons. I know John was pretty excited at the time. I think we had Anthony Miller and Mike Pritchard. I know the Broncos went all out to try and get John surrounded with a lot of weapons. We had Shannon [Sharpe]. We had a really good offense. We traded for Gary Zimmerman from Minnesota. Mr. Bowlen and the football guys, they were all, 'We're going to give John every tool he's always dreamed of.' At least, I think that was the hope. Just general excitement. I remember my first training camp and being out at practice with these guys and seeing what they could do. My thought process was, *Look at the talent we have here.*"

Usually, when a team changes its head coach, it goes 180 degrees from the man who just got fired. After 10 years of Elway having a difficult time getting along with head coach Dan Reeves, owner Pat Bowlen wanted to make sure his quarterback felt as comfortable as possible. He couldn't sway Elway's first choice as head coach, Mike Shanahan, to start the 1993 season, but he came up with more than a few consolation gifts.

Wade Phillips, the son of Bum Phillips, the popular head coach of the Houston Oilers in the 1980s and a college and NFL defensive coach for 24 years, had more than proven himself ready to become a full-time head coach.

Phillips' experience included 12 years as an NFL defensive coordinator, mostly notably the 1989–92 seasons as head of the Broncos' defense.

In contrast to the ever-intense Reeves, Phillips was a folksy, friendly sort who could quickly deliver a quip. "Wade was just awesome to be around," Elam said. "He was a players' coach. He treated us very well. He was funny. He made it fun. It was a big transition for me, going from college to pros and trying to get used to all that. But I remember thinking, *I'm going to have a lot of chances.* The offense is going to move the ball, and I'm going to be kicking extra points. They're going to put me in position to kick field goals. We're not going to punt a lot. Not just that year but every year that John was there."

Indeed, the Broncos in their first year under Phillips/Fassel finished No. 3 in the 28-team NFL in scoring, matching the 1973 Broncos under John Ralston for best ranking in team history. One of the first steps Bowlen and Phillips made to appease Elway was to hire Jim Fassel as his offensive coordinator.

Fassel was an assistant coach at Stanford all four years Elway played quarterback for the Cardinal, coaching receivers and running backs in 1979–80 and serving as offensive coordinator in 1981–82. Fassel ran the West Coast offensive system—with even numbers to the right, by the way, odd numbers to the left. "We did a lot better offensively," Elway said in November 2023 of the first season with Fassel as the Broncos' offensive coordinator. "We had some good years with my stat numbers. That went back to when I was in the West Coast coming out, what we did at Stanford. Jim was my coach for years at Stanford. So I had a good relationship with him. I liked that offense a lot. Everything was tied into your feet, the drops, tight end move. What we were doing in college made what we had been doing here look antiquated."

Two more moves were made besides Fassel. One, Bowlen hired Elway's father, Jack, as a pro scout. A longtime college head coach and offensive coordinator, Jack had spent two years as the Frankfort Galaxy's head coach in 1991–92 when Bowlen summoned. As it turned out, Jack Elway was a bonding bridge of sorts between his son and the rookie kicker. "John was awesome to me," Elam said. "My understanding was it was his dad who really advocated for me. Jack had scouted me and had put in a good word. His whole thing was, 'Find a good kicker and stick with him.' He told me that over and over, Jack did. 'Find a good kicker and stick with him.'

"And so I don't know if Jack talked to John about why they took a kicker in the third round, but John was always great to me. He was very steady. That was the thing about John's personality was he never got low, and he never got over-the-top high. He was just a constant for us, very encouraging. I never heard him say anything negative to any of my teammates.

He was always incredibly encouraging. He was the first one out to tap me on a field goal or congratulate me and he was right there celebrating with all of us."

There would be one more move Bowlen and the Broncos would make before the 1993 season that was Elway favorable—trading for Minnesota Vikings left tackle Gary Zimmerman. A four-time Pro Bowler and two-time, first-team All-Pro, Zimmerman became disenchanted with the Vikings' 10-person board of directors who ran the organization. The penny-pinching Vikings board even put timers on the showers and charged players if they had to replace lost socks.

The final straw for Zimmerman was when he asked the board for an advance on some of his deferred money for tax purposes. A board member insulted him instead, and Zimmerman vowed he would retire rather than play for the 10 people in charge. He sat out training camp and the first three preseason games before the Vikings dealt him to the Broncos prior to the last preseason game of 1993. Frustrated that his team had gone through six left tackles in the five years since Dave Studdard blew out his knee in Super Bowl XXII, the Broncos went after Zimmerman on the advice of trusted scouts Jerry Frei and Jack Elway.

The Broncos sent a substantial haul—first-, second- and sixth-round draft picks—to Minnesota in exchange for

Zimmerman. But it was worth the significant cost. Elway's blind side would now be well-protected. "They were trying to trade me to the Jets to stick it to me because they knew I didn't like New York," Zimmerman said in *50 Greatest Players in Denver Broncos History*. "But nothing happened there. They called me and said Denver would like you, and I was on a plane the next day."

After the Broncos went 8–8 in their previous 1992 season under Reeves, they were 9–5 with two games remaining in Phillips' first season of 1993. The Broncos then lost to the Tampa Bay Buccaneers 17–10 at home before blowing a 30–13 second-half lead to the Los Angeles Raiders to fall 33–30 in overtime. That left the Broncos with a 9–7 record that was good enough to qualify for the AFC playoffs as a wild-card, but it also meant an immediate return trip to Los Angeles to play the Raiders in the Los Angeles Coliseum. Elway was outstanding in the first-round playoff game, throwing three touchdowns all in the first half and for 307 yards, but the Raiders' Napoleon McCallum rushed for three second-half touchdowns, and the Raiders won going away 42–24.

Elway finished with the best statistical season of his career in 1993, leading the NFL with 348 completions, 551 attempts, and 4,030 yards—the only time in his 16-year career he eclipsed 4,000 yards. He also completed a career-best 63.2 percent of his passes for a career-most 25 touchdowns with a career-low 10 interceptions. All of those numbers computed to a career-best 92.8 passer rating.

He would later surpass his 25 touchdown passes in each of his first three seasons with Shanahan as his coach and play caller from 1995 to 1997. But with Elway playing the best of his career in 1993, the Broncos doubled down on offense for the 1994 season by signing four-time Pro Bowler Miller from free agency and the rival San Diego Chargers and trading for Pritchard, the former University of Colorado standout who was coming off 77 and 74 catch seasons with the Atlanta Falcons. The 1993 season is also when Sharpe made the leap from Pro Bowl tight end to first team All-Pro with 81 catches for 995 yards and nine touchdowns. He was then sensational in the playoff game against the Raiders, compiling 13 catches for 156 yards and another touchdown.

The Broncos were all in for the 1994 season. But then they began 0–4.

They were 1–5 after losing that Monday night heartbreaker to Montana and the Chiefs, but to Phillips' credit, the Broncos rallied to win six of their next seven games to move to 7–6. The Broncos could have made the playoffs for a second time in two seasons under Phillips had they won two of their last three games. But Elway injured his left knee in a Game 13 rematch win at Kansas City. He missed two of the last three games and couldn't make it through the other, including a blowout, 42–19 loss to none other than Shanahan and the San Francisco 49ers. Although backup quarterback Hugh Millen played fairly well in the final three games, the Broncos lost all three.

With a 7–9 record, Phillips and much of his coaching staff were doomed, especially with Shanahan and the 49ers about to trounce everyone in their postseason way to capture Super Bowl XXIX, culminating their dominant season with a 49–26 shellacking of the Chargers that wasn't that close. (San Francisco was up 42–10 midway through the third quarter.)

As the Broncos cleaned out their lockers the day after Christmas, Elway delivered a somber eulogy on the 1994 season. "I think we're a ways away," Elway told reporters at his locker. "Everyone talks about the Super Bowl around here. We better start talking about getting to the playoffs and winning a couple of playoff games. I think that as disappointing as this season has been, everyone's just as disappointed that we didn't play better for Wade. For him to be in this position with what's being said, who knows what's going to happen? Everyone's disappointed we didn't play better because, even though Wade takes most of the responsibility or is responsible for it, I think that we all have to be accountable for the way we played. That's the disappointing thing at least through my eyes. We didn't play better than we did. If we had played to our capabilities, none of this would be happening right now."

On December 29, 1994, Phillips was fired along with most of his coaching staff. "I had lost confidence in the coaching staff," Bowlen said in announcing the firing.

All that remained was for the 49ers to finish their postseason run so Bowlen could bring Shanahan back as head coach. Bowlen would have to wait a full 31 days until the 49ers disposed of the Chargers in Super Bowl XXIX. But not an hour more. Bowlen all but locked up Shanahan at the team hotel after the game.

In just four years, Shanahan transformed the Broncos into back-to-back world champions. Phillips, though, had reason to feel he was a contributor. Phillips, general manager John Beake, and director of player personnel Bob Ferguson had acquired Zimmerman in a trade, selected running back/returner Glyn Milburn and Elam early in the 1993 draft, and drafted linebacker Allen Aldridge early in the 1994 draft. Then they hit it big at the tail end of that 1994 draft. In the seventh round, the Broncos took linebacker and special teams standout Keith Burns; center Tom Nalen, who would go on to become the best offensive lineman in Broncos history; and signed an undrafted, 24-year-old rookie receiver out of Missouri Southern named Rod Smith.

Smith spent the entire 1994 season on the Broncos' practice squad, but he wound up becoming the Broncos' all-time leading receiver in every significant category. Smith still holds those career records. That's pretty impressive for anyone—let alone for someone who redshirted in 1994. "I was grateful," Smith said. "The practice squad, I needed it. I really did. I was just glad. Coach Fassel and Coach Wade—still to this day when I run into Coach Wade, I say thank you because he gave me a chance to be on the practice squad."

One other subtle improvement Phillips and Fassel accomplished during their two years leading the Broncos was that they unshackled Elway's spirit, freeing him to become the undisputed leader of the Broncos' franchise. "To me John was a consummate professional," Smith said in recalling his rookie season of 1994. "I didn't know how to be a pro when I first came in. It started with John, but it was more directly with Shannon. John was the figurehead of the entire region. I still remember my first time as a rookie, jumping in to spell somebody on probably a run play and I'm in the same huddle as John Elway. It felt amazing for me, a kid who grew up in the projects, went to a small school six years, and had all these injuries, and here I'm in the huddle with John Elway my rookie year. It might have been mop-up work, but John was in the huddle. I was in the huddle with John Elway."

Elway was always a leader. It's just he no longer had to look over his shoulder to see Reeves' imposing shadow. "It was a kick I missed my rookie year," Elam said. "I was sitting in the locker room afterward, going over in my head what went wrong, and John came over and pulled a chair up behind me and sat down and said, 'Hey, we drafted you for a reason. You're going to be in this league for a long time. I believe in you, the team believes in you. And don't worry about it.' It was that kind of leadership where I was like, 'Man, I'm going to work my tail off and do everything in my power not to let that guy down.'"

Elway was the man. But even the top guy needed guidance. Bowlen was about to make the best hire of his 35-year career as Broncos owner. He was about to make Shanahan his next head coach.

CHAPTER SIX

THE MASTERMIND

After Dan Reeves was fired following the 1992 season, Denver Broncos owner Pat Bowlen's first replacement choice was Mike Shanahan. To Bowlen's surprise, Shanahan turned him down. Bowlen fired Reeves after 12 seasons as Broncos head coach in part because the owner was sure he could make Shanahan—his all-time favorite assistant coach—the new football boss. The NFL's Rooney Rule, which required teams to interview minority candidates for head coaching positions, was still 11 years away.

Absent the Rooney Rule, Bowlen had one man in mind to become his first head coaching hire. (Remember Bowlen inherited Reeves when he and his two siblings bought a majority stake in the Broncos from Edgar Kaiser Jr. for $51 million in 1984.) Bowlen's master plan was waylaid, though, when Shanahan, who had become a close friend in his years as an offensive assistant, balked for a couple reasons. One, even in the position of lower-paid (but still well-paid) offensive coordinator and not a head coach, you couldn't beat working for the San Francisco 49ers. Team owner Eddie DeBartolo Jr. treated everyone in the organization with class—and not just the players and coaches. There was first-class travel with chef-prepared meals. While almost every team had their players double up in hotel rooms on the road, 49ers players got their own rooms. Breakfast and lunch meals were served at the team's practice facility, not just dinner.

And they won, too. Won big. George Seifert was in his fourth season as Bill Walsh's head coach successor in 1992 and he did a great job of continuing on the organizational culture his predecessor had established. With Shanahan as Seifert's first-year offensive coordinator in 1992, the 49ers went 14–2 to earn a first-round playoff bye and led the NFL in scoring with 26.9 points per game. They lost to the Dallas Cowboys in the first of three consecutive NFC Championship Game matchups, but Shanahan was immersed in the 49ers' methods.

Still, he talked with Bowlen who was offering Shanahan the chance to leave San Francisco after one season and succeed Reeves as Broncos head coach for the 1993 season. Much to the disappointment of star quarterback John Elway, Shanahan declined. He explained:

"When Pat Bowlen asked me to come back after the '92 season, he asked me to come back and be the head coach, and I told Pat the things I felt we needed to win a Super Bowl. He said, 'Well, I can't give you that in writing.' And I said, 'If not, I'm going to stay in San Francisco.' He said, 'You won't do that. You're too close to John.' I said, 'One of the reasons why I won't do it is I *am* close to John. I know how important it is that if I do come back to Denver, we've got to win Super Bowls. We just can't go to the game. We've got to win it because I knew how the fans felt and how I felt when I was there and being embarrassed in those Super Bowls, even though we went there.'"

What did Shanahan require from Bowlen? Huge financial commitments to begin with. The hottest topics in the NFL were the advent of unrestricted free agency in 1993 and a salary cap system in 1994. In its constant negotiating battles with the players union, the NFL in 1989 came up with a Plan B free agency system in which each of the 28 teams could assert exclusive rights to 37 veteran players on their roster. Freeman McNeil, a New York Jets running back in his 12th (and as it turned out final) season, was among the Plan Bs. He led a lawsuit filed by seven players against Plan B. It took three years for the legal system to play out, but in 1992 a federal jury ruled Plan B violated antitrust laws. The result was team owners and the players' union negotiated a new collective bargaining agreement that allowed unrestricted free agency to begin in 1993—a win for the players—with a salary cap system implemented in 1994—a compromise for the owners.

If Bowlen wanted Shanahan to be his head coach in 1992, the owner had to promise in writing the Broncos would spend to the salary cap ceiling every year. To show how exploding

TV revenues beginning in 1994 changed the NFL's economy, the initial 1994 salary cap was $34.6 million. Cowboys quarterback Troy Aikman was the NFL's highest-paid player with an average contract of $6.25 million per year. In 2023 the NFL's salary cap was $224.8 million—a 649 percent increase over 30 years—while Cincinnati Bengals quarterback Joe Burrow was the highest-paid player with a $55 million per year average. Burrow was among five quarterbacks making at least $51 million on average in 2023, and there were 15 quarterbacks with contracts averaging at least $35 million a year—more than a team's entire salary capped payroll in 1994.

The revenue explosion could not have been fully predicted, but whatever the salary ceiling was, Shanahan wanted his Broncos to hit it. "At least be in the top 10," Shanahan said. "And I told Pat I want to be in the top 10 with coaches' salaries. I wanted meals for the players—breakfast and lunch—so I can have these guys hanging out at the facility. And the other thing is: I wanted players to have their own [hotel] rooms because I found out in San Francisco that one of the biggest things for our players was they needed to get a good night's sleep especially the day before the game. I said I'll pay for it."

Bowlen, who always operated on the thinnest of margins to the point he once had to take out a loan to sign veteran free-agent Simeon Rice in 2007, couldn't completely commit to what would be significant added expenses. So Shanahan went back to the 49ers; he never told Elway why he didn't take the Broncos' job. Instead, he told Elway a little white lie that he and Bowlen couldn't reach an agreement on salary. The reason why Shanahan didn't tell Elway the truth about needing so many team-beneficial requirements in writing was he didn't want the quarterback to become upset with his owner. That could have caused irreconcilable differences between Elway and Bowlen. Shanahan had his fill with the Elway-Reeves squabbles. He didn't need to eventually return to the team and find Elway and Bowlen weren't happy with each other. "Pat didn't have a lot of money to do what Mike wanted," Elway said. "But Mike wouldn't tell me the reason he turned Pat down. He told me it was salary, and I said, 'Well, what's the difference?' He goes, 'Ah, ah, ah $250,000, $500,000.' I said, 'I'll pay ya. I'll pay you the difference to come coach us.' And he goes, 'Aaahh, Aaahh, Aaahh.'" Elway laughed.

Spurned by Shanahan following the 1992 season, Bowlen turned to his own defensive coordinator Wade Phillips to replace Reeves as head coach, which worked out okay. Not great, but not bad. The Broncos went to the playoffs their first season under Phillips albeit with a slightly better than average 9–7 record. But Bowlen wanted better. He wanted what Shanahan had in San Francisco. Shanahan's 49ers offense again led the NFL in scoring in 1993—this time with a 29.6 points per game average—2.63 points more than their league-leading scoring total in 1992—and again received a first-round playoff bye and again won a second-round divisional playoff game. And once again, San Francisco lost to the Cowboys in the NFC Championship Game.

The third time, though, was the charm. The 49ers behind Steve Young, Jerry Rice, and Deion Sanders—the league's undisputed top cornerback who was in his first and only year with the team—would not be denied. The 49ers went 13–3 in the regular season with Young topping Lions running back Barry Sanders for the NFL's Most Valuable Player award.

For the third time in three years with Shanahan as their offensive coordinator, the 49ers led the league in scoring— this time with a whopping 31.6 points per game. After their first-round playoff bye, the 49ers crushed the Chicago Bears 44–15 in the NFC divisional round and finally whipped the Cowboys 38–28 in the NFC Championship Game. It wasn't that close. The unstoppable 49ers jumped out to a 21–0 lead and were up 31–14 at halftime before coasting the rest of the way. In Super Bowl XXIX, Young threw six touchdown passes in a 49–24 romp against the San Diego Chargers.

The 49ers were a top six rushing team each of Shanahan's three years there and led the league with 4.8 and 4.6 yards per carry in 1992 and '93. Not easy to do when Young and Rice were at the same time compiling passing records. "Everyone talked about the 49ers passing game," Shanahan said of the early 1990 offenses he directed. "But those three years, what made them different was their running game."

Shanahan had reached the Mount Everest of football mountain tops, albeit as an offensive coordinator, not a head coach. He was ready again for that final step as head coach— only this time not with unpredictable owner Al Davis and the Raiders, as he did in 1988 and four games into 1989—but with the owner and organization of his NFL roots, Bowlen and the Broncos. After the 49ers' Super Bowl win in Miami, who would be waiting for Shanahan after the game in the lobby of their team hotel? Bowlen. He was ready to put Shanahan's requests—top 10 in salary cap, top 10 in assistant coaches' salaries, single rooms for players, breakfast and lunch at the team facility—in writing.

Bowlen got his man. Shanahan became the ninth head coach in Broncos history starting with the 1995 season. "I remember everybody being excited about Mike, just being such an offensive genius," said kicker Jason Elam, who had just completed his second season with the Broncos. "We were playing the 49ers the year before, and they handled us pretty good. They had so many weapons all over the place. They had Steve Young and Rice and Taylor and their tight end, Brent Jones, and they were running up and down the field on us. Roger Craig. Somebody was wide open the whole time. You couldn't cover everybody. I remember everybody being excited that he was going to get us over the hump. And this is going to be a really fun run. Coach Shanahan was much different than Wade. It was a respect, and we respected Wade, too, but we were—what's the word I'm looking for?—a little more fearful of Coach Shanahan. There was a professionalism and there was a certain way that you had to approach every second in practice, not just the game. Every second in practice. You crossed that line walking on the field, you better have your focus. They were highly organized, and at the same time, he really went to bat for us as players. The meals, having breakfast, having a better lunch, staying at very, very nice hotels, it wasn't like we were all crammed in listening to each other snore before a game. So there was a standard where Coach Shanahan said, 'I'm going to treat you guys as well as I possibly can and I'm going to make sure you're ready every Sunday to walk on the field. In return, I'm expecting you to give me, your teammates, the organization, and the fanbase everything you've got.' That really resonated."

What Bowlen didn't know when he hired Shanahan was he was about to get a two-for-one deal. Gary Kubiak had retired as Elway's backup quarterback following his strong performance in the AFC Championship Game in Buffalo to cap Denver's 1991 season and became an assistant coach for his alma mater Texas A&M in 1992–93. He was hired by Shanahan as San Francisco's quarterbacks coach in 1994 with the idea of replacing Shanahan as the 49ers' offensive coordinator when Shanny got his next head coaching gig. "After '93 George [Seifert] wanted to bring an offensive coach to replace me as coordinator in case I got a head coaching job the next year," Shanahan said. "So I brought in Gary."

As it turned out when the moment of truth arrived, Kubiak's loyalty was to Shanahan and Denver much more than the 49ers. "I had been there a year with Mike, and we won the Super Bowl with Steve Young, and Mike gets the Broncos' job right after the game," Kubiak said in 2023. "Mr. Bowlen, I see him at the hotel. Things are going down pretty quick. The 49ers tried to get me to stay, and at that time, being a coordinator for the 49ers was kind of a fast track to getting an NFL [head coaching] opportunity, but my loyalty and ties to Mike and John and my family loving Denver, it was easy for me to say, 'No, I'm coming with you. Let's go.' That was a dream come true for me, and I had a lot of work to do before I was going to get to a [head coaching] opportunity and I knew that. So going with Mike was the best thing for me to do."

There was one other lesson Shanahan learned from the 49ers that he brought with him in his third return stint with the Broncos: bringing every single employee together to work as one organization with the common goal of winning the Super Bowl. Not just coaches and players. Everybody who works for a team. It helped create an environment where the night custodian could chitchat with the coach watching late-night film, the administrative assistants could say hello to the person selling ads in the gameday program, and the ticket taker felt as important in her job as the placekicker did in his. "The other thing I told Pat was what the 49ers had done that we had never done here was the attention to detail with the support staff, the ground crew, the training staff, the doctors," Shanahan said. "We met my first day in San Francisco for 10 hours. There were no coaches in there except for me because I was the new guy as the offensive coordinator. I listened to everybody's role in the organization. We didn't talk one thing about football, 10 to 12 hours. That was a great learning experience for me. George was explaining that everyone has to be ranked in the top five. George told me if I wasn't in the top five on offense, we'd probably have to let you go because to win Super Bowls we're going to need the best at every position and not just the coaching staff but the support staff as well. When I was done with that meeting, it was so impressive to me I said to myself, 'Now I know why this team has won four Super Bowls in nine years.' [The Broncos] had been to three Super Bowls in four years. But this [San Francisco] team had been to four

Super Bowls in nine years and had won them all. Coaching football was something that had come naturally to me. I had studied different college teams and pro teams. But the one thing I never had was knowing the roles and responsibilities of everybody in the organization."

Remember when Shanahan told Bowlen he would pay the difference between double-occupied hotel rooms and singles? That was the agreement as Shanahan's first Broncos team of 1995 took off for their first preseason road trip at San Francisco followed the next week with a visit to the Carolina Panthers. "I didn't even tell my wife about that," Shanahan said. "If I told my wife, she would have thought I was crazy. She would have never allowed it. So I never told my wife."

But then the bill came due. "Pat took care of it," Shanahan said.

Shanahan would never get another bill. By then Bowlen had split his responsibilities between overseeing all football and business aspects of the Broncos while also serving as cochairman of NFL broadcast committee. Bowlen was instrumental in bringing in a third network, FOX, to carry NFL games on Sunday while NBC concentrated on delivering its primetime Sunday night broadcast package. TV revenues soared for the NFL and expanded the coffers for its 28 teams. Bowlen could afford single hotel rooms, daily breakfast and lunch for the players, and have enough left over for his tailored suits and high-fashion cowboy boots.

Once the pertinent details with his owner and friend were worked out, Shanahan next had to sell his quarterback on the plan. And the plan with the ultimate goal of winning the Super Bowl—not merely getting to the Big Game but winning it—was essentially to build an offense that was slightly less about Elway and more about running the ball.

* * *

For his first meeting with John Elway as head coach, Mike Shanahan wisely used Dan Marino as an example. Elway and Marino were quarterback rivals, even though their teams rarely faced each other over their respective long careers. They were rivals, though, because they were both first-round picks in the 1983 NFL Draft. Elway was the No. 1 overall selection and the first of six quarterbacks taken in the first round; Marino slumped in his senior year at Pitt, throwing more interceptions (22) than touchdowns (17), and was the sixth and last quarterback taken in the first round (No. 27 overall) when Don Shula's Miami Dolphins selected him.

Marino played in a much more passer-friendly offense and took to the NFL game more quickly. In only his second season of 1984, he delivered a historic passing performance with a record 48 touchdowns and 5,084 yards. It wasn't until 20 years later that Peyton Manning broke Marino's touchdown record with 49 in 2004. Marino's single-season passing yardage marker wasn't surpassed for another 27 years until Drew Brees and Tom Brady both took advantage of the NFL's pass-friendly rule changes. Marino led the Dolphins to the only Super Bowl game in his career in 1984—only to get trounced by Joe Montana's San Francisco 49ers 38–16.

Wearing loafers with no socks, jeans, and a sweater, Shanahan was seated at a table in his otherwise empty Shanahan's steakhouse restaurant in the Denver Tech Center in October 2023, talking about that 49ers–Dolphins Super Bowl. "Guess how many times the Dolphins ran the ball?" Shanahan rhetorically asked. "Nine times for 25 yards. How many times did Marino throw the ball? 50. Joe Montana, I think, was 24-of-35, ran the ball 40 times for 211 yards."

Amazing. Here was Shanahan sitting at his restaurant at 71 years old, and his memory was so sharp that it was as if he was reading the Super Bowl XIX box score from a sheet of paper in front of him. Nearly 40 years earlier, the Dolphins did indeed run the ball exactly nine times for 25 yards. The 49ers rushed exactly 40 times for 211 yards. Montana completed exactly 24 of 35, as Shanahan said from the top of his head. Marino did indeed throw it 50 times. "Dan Marino set all the passing records that year, but he only got 25 yards rushing and he got embarrassed because they got beat by [22] points in the Super Bowl," Shanahan said.

Perhaps the reason why Shanahan could so specifically recite the stats from that game was it became the center point in his first address to Elway about the new way the Broncos would play offensive football. "I told John, I said, 'John, you might not be in the Pro Bowl. I think you will, but we've been to Super Bowls because of your ability to make plays,'" Shanahan said. "I told him, 'The only way we're going to win one is if I get you a good running game.' He said, 'I'll do anything you want. I'll take any chance I can as long as we win a Super Bowl. I don't care how many times we run it. I've been to three and got our ass kicked, and it's more embarrassing than anything.'"

When Elway went to his first Super Bowl to cap the 1986 season, the Broncos averaged 3.7 yards per carry. For his second Super Bowl to finish 1987, they averaged 3.9 yards per carry. Two years later for Elway's third Super Bowl appearance in the 1989 season, the Broncos averaged 3.8 yards per carry. Elway could get the Broncos there, but he didn't have enough of a running game to control the line of scrimmage against the more physical NFC champions in the Super Bowl.

Elway's reaction to learning there would be more running the ball and relying less on him all in the name of winning the Super Bowl from his first meeting with Shanahan? "Yeah.

I didn't care," Elway said. "Winning the Super Bowl was what I was still chasing, and I liked the offense. I knew what the base was. I was like, 'Whatever you need me to do, I'll do.'"

As for Elway himself, he wasn't quite as spry following his 12th season of 1994 as when Shanahan first joined the Broncos as an offensive assistant in 1984. Elway had just been sacked a league-most 46 times in just 14 games in 1994, which left him with 416 in his career to that point. Maybe his fastball had dropped a couple miles an hour from when he fired that ball into Mark Jackson to finish The Drive in the 1986 AFC Championship Game.

But he still had all the arm strength he needed and then some. "He had reached that point in his career where we were having to manage some things," said Gary Kubiak, who had become Elway's offensive coordinator, not his backup quarterback buddy. "Damn, he had played so many years and was beat on so much. So Mike had put a great plan in place to how he was going to manage John's offseason workload, all those things to keep a player motivated so you can get another two or three great years out of him because while there was no doubt John still wanted to play and compete—that was a no-brainer—but there are some things that go along with that, the hours in the offseason, the meetings. There are some ways where you want to make it a lot of fun for guys like that once they reach that point in their careers to keep them motivated, to keep them going. And to be honest with you, listening to John helped us coach him. We were both his friends obviously, but now we were in different roles, having to do a job and we needed to listen to him and where he was mentally, physically, personally so that we could put that thing together for him where he could go out and win us a couple championships."

Shanahan finished off his initial meeting as head coach with Elway by hammering home the message he first emphasized. "'If I can get you a running game and a good defense, you'll have better stats than you had at any point in your career,'" Shanahan said. "But I said, 'You have to have faith No. 1, and it may take us a year to do it.'"

Elway was all in.

It did take Shanahan a year to get his roster and culture formed to his vision. Sitting at 7–6 with three games remaining in the 1995 season, the Broncos finished by losing back-to-back close games to AFC West rivals Seattle Seahawks as John Friesz—*John Friesz!*—threw two fourth-quarter touchdown passes to erase a 27–17 deficit and win 31–27 and then to the division champion Kansas City Chiefs 20–17 in Arrowhead Stadium.

The Broncos were 7–8 and out of the postseason hunt. "It was a brand-new system," said Mark Schlereth, the Broncos left guard who came over from Washington via free agency prior to the 1995 season. "When you're installing a brand-new system, especially with the quarterback, you don't know what you don't like until you get your ass kicked doing it. Every experience is new. Every read has a little different nuance. So you might get to the red zone early in the season and you throw a pick you don't know [what] you didn't like about that play until you find out. I think we finished that season fairly strong. We beat the Raiders 27–0 on a Monday Night here at home and then beating the Raiders again the last game of the season. So I think we finished with some confidence. We lost to Kansas City, but I think we played really well. I always felt if you went on the road against Kansas City and played a close game, you were a pretty good football team. So those little things stacked one on top of the other."

The Broncos did win their season finale 31–28 against the hated Raiders in Oakland after Elway put together one of his patented, fourth-quarter comebacks from a 28–17 deficit. "The difference in those eras was organization," said receiver Rod Smith, who went from practice squad rookie with Wade Phillips and Jim Fassel in 1994 to the Broncos' all-time receiving leader by the time he played his last game in 2006. "We weren't as organized in the Wade Phillips and Jim Fassel era as we were in the Shanahan era. We had talented guys, but you could tell it was more a team of individuals. Everybody was focused on themselves versus everybody focusing on us as a group with Mike Shanahan. And I think even Mr. Bowlen changed when Mike Shanahan changed the culture. I think if Mr. Bowlen continued to run it the way he was running it, we would have never won the Super Bowl. You had coaches that basically didn't come with the structure.

"And so for John, statistically he may have went down in some ways, but to see him acting like a 12-year-old kid playing football in the backyard with a friend was during the Shanahan era. It wasn't as strenuous on him because he didn't have to do everything. And you saw him have more fun. And I personally witnessed John going through that time where he just enjoyed playing football. I took that from him—play with this passion like you did when you were 12. When Coach Shanahan came, you could see all the guys that left. We didn't win immediately because the structure had to get fixed. And Mr. Bowlen gave him the resources to fix the structure. The structure wasn't just about physical talent. It was mental, it was emotional, it was all those other things that make a team great. And I saw John transition with Coach Shanahan and Kubes, who said, 'Let's make this game fun for him by taking some pressure off of him, but he's still going to be a first-ballot Hall of Famer and dominant quarterback in the NFL with less stats.' And I think that's what happened."

Although the Broncos finished 8–8 in 1995, there was much to build on. Some important pieces were put in place.

One was Schlereth. Raised in Alaska he played his college ball at the University of Idaho and then became a 10th-round selection of the then-Washington Redskins in the 1989 draft. He was a six-year starting right guard for Washington, a second-wave member of the Hogs. He made the Pro Bowl in 1991 when Washington went 14–2 with Mark Rypien at quarterback and Joe Gibbs as head coach. The Redskins capped that year by dominating the Buffalo Bills in Super Bowl XXVI.

A free agent after the 1994 season, Schlereth initially struggled to land a job. It wasn't from a lack of interest. Beat up so much during his 12-year playing career that he underwent 29 surgeries—including 15 on his left knee, five on his right—Schlereth couldn't find a team to pass him on his physical exam. The Chicago Bears, Indianapolis Colts, and Atlanta Falcons all wanted him, but their respective medical teams flunked him on his physical.

In 1993 with Washington, Schlereth lost feeling in his arms and legs and didn't play well through the first nine games before he had to shut it down the rest of the season. He started off the 1994 season 25 pounds underweight. But then as he began to gradually gain weight, he started playing well again by the end of that season. Pete Rodriguez, Washington's special teams coach, was good friends with new Broncos offensive line coach Alex Gibbs, who had come over to join Shanahan's staff from Kansas City. Gibbs and Shanahan had worked on Dan Reeves' staff in Denver from 1984 to 1987.

Gibbs liked Schlereth as a player, and Rodriguez told him the guard was healthy again.

"Alex sold Shanahan on my physical," Schlereth said in October 2023. "He said, 'We've got to manage him, but this guy can play.' I came in to do a physical with the Broncos doctors and I could have made fart noises with my arm pits, and they would have passed me. They didn't care. I had already passed the physical before I took the physical."

As a left guard, Schlereth had nine-year starter and future Hall of Famer Gary Zimmerman on his left and first-year starting center Tom Nalen on his right and Elway behind him. In Washington, Schlereth blocked for a merry-go-round of quarterbacks: Rypien, Doug Williams, Stan Humphries, Rich Gannon, Heath Shuler, Friesz, Gus Frerotte. All had their moments, but none matched the status of the latest quarterback he would be protecting in Denver.

Schlereth, like every other free agent who signed with the Broncos in the 1990s, did so in no small part because Elway was the quarterback. Schlereth remembers his impression of Elway while he was playing for Washington and his first impression of Elway when he became his new teammate. "You knew he was an NFL superstar, legend. So you watched him," Schlereth said. "As a player on another team, he's one of those guys you would watch. As an offensive lineman coming in—kind of being a fly on the wall, not try to be buddy-buddy with anybody, just trying to work it—one thing I always said about John is he earned the right in the eyes of the world to be a prima donna, and he never was one. Not like we ever hung out and had beers. We never did. I didn't drink. So it wasn't anything like that, but I always respected the fact that he was a guy who could say, 'I'm not doing that today or I'm not coming in today' but never did. Always ran.

"I'll never forget we're doing this Hammer Leg Press. It was the offseason where'd they break us off into groups of five. It was miserable, and Rich Tuten was the strength coach and he's leaning on this machine. You're shaking. You leave it and you can hardly stand up. It was just miserable. I'll never forget I'm in the group with John, and John sits in that Hammer Leg Press machine and he looks at Rich Tuten and says, 'You realize if I decline and not do it, I'm still going to make the team. You do know that, right?' We're all laughing because it's true. He's still making the team. And then he went ahead like everybody else and paid his penance and did the exercise. Mondays, if we lost and we had to get together with the team, John's right there running with everybody else."

That was how Schlereth remembered Elway going into the season. Once the games began, the guard became familiar with

Elway's leadership style. Let's just say it was more Southern California brand than Marino's Western Pennsylvania. "John never yelled at us in the huddle, never screamed," Schlereth said. "The only time he raised his voice is if we got a play in late and we had to get it snapped. 'Hurry up, we've got to go, go, go.' But there was always just a quiet confidence when he walked in the huddle. We always had that feeling of we got them right where we want them. We could be down 14 and we thought, *That's nothing. Fourteen is nothing.* You always felt that way when he walked in the huddle."

Elway in his 13th NFL season—and his first with Shanahan as his head coach—threw a career-best 26 touchdown passes in 1995. Most notably, the Broncos introduced a sixth-round running back out of Georgia named Terrell Davis, who rushed for 1,117 yards as a rookie, even though he missed the final two-and-a-half games with a torn hamstring. Elway at 35 years old was playing some of his best football and was clearly invigorated. After all, handing it off to T.D. and watching the strong, slashing running back make his one-cut runs behind the Broncos' zone-blocking system would energize the most veteran of quarterbacks.

CHAPTER SEVEN

T.D.

For all the highlight-reel runs, awards, and records Terrell Davis compiled mostly over a four-year span during his Pro Football Hall of Fame career, the story most often told in the years since he retired was about a tackle—a tackle he made on special teams. "I know. It's crazy," Davis said in November 2023. "That first year was cool."

Not at first. A sixth-round draft pick out of Georgia in 1995, Davis wasn't getting many reps during training camp. In the first preseason game against the 49ers in San Francisco, he was the sixth running back in. He got just one carry, and that didn't occur until there were about six minutes left in the game. He ran off left guard and got stuffed for no gain.

After that game was finished on Saturday, July 29, the Denver Broncos and 49ers both flew off to Tokyo for preseason game No. 2. As the week went on, Davis became more and more depressed. *Camp meat* is how he was describing his situation. Davis figured he was the No. 6 or 7 running back on the depth chart. Aaron Craver, Reggie Rivers, Glyn Milburn, Derrick Clark, and Sheldon Canley all got carries before Davis did in the preseason opener in San Francisco. Rod Bernstine, an eight-year veteran, was coming back from a severe knee injury and was held out, though he was assured of a spot on the team once he proved himself healthy.

As Davis was sitting around his hotel room nearly 6,000 air miles from Denver, he got the idea to fly home. Leave the team, go home, and find something else to do with his life besides football. "If he'd been able to speak Japanese," Elway recalled nearly three decades later, "he would have been gone."

Davis called down to the front desk about the possibility of flying back to Denver—which would have meant the end of his NFL career—but he and the front desk person couldn't understand each other's language. He gave up on the thought, went back to staring at the ceiling in his hotel room, and was in meetings and on the team bus to practice the next day. "I wasn't getting reps with the team," Davis said. "I was getting rookie reps. I watched everybody else get reps. I didn't play in the first preseason game. I wasn't starting on any special teams. And then the limited amount of reps I was getting, I remember [running backs coach] Bobby Turner was constantly on me. Alignment things. I used to wear my pants halfway down my butt, and he used to get on me about that. The way I dressed, alignment issues. I think I was decent with alignments, might have blown one here and there, but the thing is, you can't blow any. If you want five reps, you can't blow one."

It was called the American Bowl, and at halftime the Japanese contest seemed like a ho-hum, typical preseason game. The Broncos were up 7–3 as Elway and the top starters came out of the game after playing three series. Davis was a long way from starting and didn't play in the first half. Davis ate a hot dog. "You're sitting on the sideline," Davis said. "I assume I'm not going to play so I'm enjoying the dog like everybody else."

Then he heard special teams coach Richard Smith bark his name. "Davis! You're in on kickoff."

Davis may or may not have had time to finish his hot dog, but he did puke it up. There was 7:01 left in the third quarter. Broncos backup quarterback Bill Musgrave had just thrown a touchdown pass to Darrick Owens, whose five catches for 78 yards and the touchdown would earn him the American Bowl's MVP. The Broncos were up 17–3.

On the ensuing kickoff, Davis was lined up to the right of kicker Jason Elam. "I talk about his story all the time—and he tells this story—he made one kickoff tackle," said Broncos receiver Rod Smith, who was trying to make the team himself after spending his previous rookie season on the practice squad. "If you see that kickoff, No. 19 was me. I'm about to tackle Tyronne Drakeford. I was right there. The MVP of that game was a receiver. He thought he had made it, and

I'm rolling on special teams, doing everything I can and I remember T.D. hit Tyronne Drakeford, and he killed him."

Drakeford caught Elam's kickoff at the 8-yard line and ran up the middle-right. He got to the 20. *WHAM!* Davis delivered a textbook blast, leading with his right shoulder pad and crushing Drakeford just above his left ribs. Drakeford did not reach the 21. Davis got up and exuberantly celebrated his blast, leaping and swinging his right arm in the air as the other special teamers led by Smith converged on him to slap him around in joyful attaboy spirit. *This was the same guy who wanted to fly home and quit?* "I remember telling myself, *Oh, he just made the team*," Elam said.

A star was born. "Coach Shanahan put his butt back at running back, and I never saw him in a special teams meeting again," Smith said before laughing. "I said, 'Ah, man, you abandoned us.' He didn't even know how to line up. I had to line his ass up. He didn't even tape his ankles."

With Davis' hit, Shanahan saw a football player. Had Davis been a linebacker, he would have played the next series. But Davis was a running back and out he went when it was time for the Broncos' next offensive series. He finished the second half with 46 yards on 11 carries. "I also threw him a slant route, and he ran it better than most of our receivers," Musgrave said years later. "And, of course, they couldn't tackle him."

In the next three preseason games in 1995, Davis added another 134 yards rushing on just 19 carries (7.1 yards per carry). He also had 106 yards on 10 catches plus returned seven kickoffs for a 26-yard average. Davis not only made the team, but also became the Broncos' first rookie running back to start Opening Day since none other than Floyd Little in 1967. Little, a first-round pick, was the Broncos' first. The future Hall of Famer later picked up the nickname of "The Franchise."

Still, Davis was unaware of his standing on the depth chart in the minutes leading up to when he was told. "The first time I took a handoff from Elway," Davis said, "I think it's Monday, and Mike calls me to his office, and I'm nervous as hell. I don't know what I did wrong. *Am I getting cut?* And Mike tells me not only did I make the team, but how do you feel about being our starting running back? I couldn't believe it. So it's Wednesday practice and it's right before we play the Bills. It's Bills week. So we go through our plays, and it's the first time I'm in the huddle with Elway. They call a play. I believe it's a *19 handoff*. We break the uddle, John goes up to the center, and I'm like, 'Holy (bleep).' It's hitting me. I'm getting some anxiety. Next thing you know John is coming toward me. *19 handoff*. And I fumble. We don't get the exchange, and the ball hits the ground. I pick it up and I run because Mike always had us run 40 yards to where Mike was standing. I ran past Mike, I jog back.

"As I'm jogging back, I see Kubiak and John talking about something. I assume it's me. Kubiak waves at me over and he says, 'John says you need to give him a bigger pocket.' So I'm like, 'Uh oh.' So we run another play, and this time I run a checkdown, about a four-yard checkdown. I'm hoping he doesn't throw me the ball, and guess what he does? He throws me a checkdown. Guess what I do? I drop it. I pick it up, I run to Mike Shanahan. And then Mike calls me over and Mike says, 'Listen, I might determine who's on this team, but No. 7 determines who plays.' That was it. I shook it off and I was good after that."

In the season and home opener against the Bills, who had won four consecutive AFC championships from 1990 to 1993 thanks to a defensive front led by Bruce Smith, Davis had a workmanlike 70 yards and a touchdown off 20 carries in a 22–7 win. He would finish the season with 1,117 yards on 4.7 per carry in just 14 games as he missed the final two-and-a-half games with a hamstring injury.

Better rookie year than he thought? "Oh yeah," Davis said. "That was one of the benefits of not being a high draft pick in that anything I did was gravy. There were no expectations. I remember Alex Gibbs in a meeting room. He kept saying, 'Just give me four yards.' I had never heard that four yards was a great run. I was always told the great runs were the 40-yard runs. No, he wanted four yards. So the hand-in-glove thing was Day One. If you had to describe me, I would say I'm a football player. I just love football. Put me at safety or maybe linebacker, whether it's true or not, in my mind I would have been equally as good at those positions. I just loved football. I played nose guard [in high school]. I played everything. I was a football player masquerading as a running back."

It's a mystery why T.D. fell to the sixth round. He began his college career at Long Beach State, but his head coach, the legendary George Allen, died after his freshman year, which served as Davis' redshirt year. Davis hung with the program for one more year under new coach Willie Brown—the same Willie Brown who was a Hall of Fame cornerback for the Broncos and Raiders in 1960s and 1970s—and averaged 4.8 yards per carry in an injury-plagued, redshirt freshman season. Long Beach State went 2–9 and decided to fold its program.

Davis had three more years of college eligibility and no college. He got a call from Georgia and was able to transfer to the SEC program without having to sit out a transfer year. He rushed for 7.3 yards a carry his first year as a sophomore in 1992, but he was the No. 3 running back behind Garrison Hearst, who rushed for 1,547 yards and 19 touchdowns to finish third in the Heisman Trophy voting (behind Gino Torretta and Marshall Faulk), and Mack Strong.

Davis' best year at Georgia was in his junior season of 1993. As the Bulldogs' No. 1 running back, he rushed for 824 yards on nearly five yards a carry. But Georgia was only 2–6 in the SEC that year. During his senior season of 1994, Davis was bothered by a nagging hamstring and only rushed for 445 yards as he had to split carries with a freshman named Hines Ward.

Davis didn't exactly have momentum going into the NFL draft. One former Broncos executive said Davis' predraft knee exams were a concern going into the draft, which explained why Davis wasn't selected until the No. 196 overall pick in the sixth round of the 1995 draft. "It wasn't that at all," Shanahan said nearly 30 years later. "He was at Georgia at the time and he didn't get some great recommendations, but we knew some people that were coaching there who said, 'Hey, whatever you're hearing is completely wrong because this guy is a great guy. We've had no problems with him.' So we got that inside information, and that's when we drafted him when we did. But we had his talent as a third- or a fourth-round draft choice."

There were 17 running backs—two named James Stewart—and four fullbacks who were drafted before Davis. One, Curtis Martin, was named the NFL's Offensive Rookie of the Year as the New England Patriots third-round pick rushed for 1,487 yards and 14 touchdowns. Davis finished second in the

Rookie of the Year voting with his 1,117 yards and seven touch-downs in two fewer games.

If there was an Offensive Second-Year Player of the Year award, it would have gone to T.D. A switch in run-game philosophy helped Davis reach another level in his second season of 1996. "That first year if you look at most of my runs, if not all of them, I'm running out of a three-point stance," Davis said. "We were running split-back formations, and most of my runs I'm running dives, I'm running traps, I'm running bombs. We didn't run the stretch zone until my second year."

After watching Davis run through his rookie season, Gibbs thought the zone-blocking system was the way to go. "I don't know why Alex thought that was a better fit," Davis said. "From watching me I don't do multiple moves, but I am a downhill guy. And in college that was a negative. I know we had some of [the one-cut zone system] my first year, but I also remember my longest run that season against the Houston Oilers. It's a dive. I'm in split-back formation, I come over the center, and it's a quick dive. So we ran some gap schemes. To stand me up in my second year and give me vision from a step back, that became a key. Man, four yards deep is great, but then you go seven? It's great."

The zone-blocking, one-cut running scheme took the NFL by storm. "If you look at what Mike did in the running game, when he got a certain type of running back—not to downplay T.D. because when he got to the secondary down-field as hard as he ran, there was no one better," Elway said. "He was a slasher. And that's what that system is: you're go, go, go and then you're downhill and then eat up as much ground as you can go."

Going forward, Davis would become the engine that would make the Broncos go. But Elway was still the driver. Elway was still the face of the franchise. And the Broncos were still his team. "I remember watching him come in when we had our OTAs and stuff, and he would walk in," Davis said. "And there's always a few people that you're always looking for when you join a team, especially a team like the Broncos. You had Steve Atwater, John Elway, I think Simon Fletcher was on the team, older guys that I knew of. So it's kind of surreal when you see them in the locker room with you. And so at first, I just watched him. I watched how he interacted with players. Because you have in your mind what you think it is, but then it's not close to what reality is. You think he gets carted in with a gold golf cart. He doesn't walk in. Your mind has a weird way of putting these people on a pedestal that doesn't come close to reality.

"The reality is John is the coolest-ass dude you ever want to be around. When I first walked in with him in the locker room, everyone was playing with him, guys were cracking jokes back and forth. It was kind of weird because I didn't expect this. I expected this dude to be like you needed a permission slip to talk to John. But from Day One, the first day I had seen him was the first day of offseason workouts, and it was voluntary. We had either a 7:00, a 10:00, and a 1:00 workout we had to go to. I go to the 10:00 workout and I'm coming in after they're finishing up the first one. We were walking in, and I stopped and watched the group in front of us. I wanted to see what they were doing. And I see a guy, no shirt on, older dude, but they were running gassers. And John was out front running gassers. I remember looking out and saying, 'Who da hell is that?' It was John. And this is after he had already established himself. He had already gone to three Super Bowls. And he's doing that at an offseason workout? That blew my mind. That's when I told himself, *Okay there's a certain way to do things. And you better watch that No. 7.*"

The Broncos were about to enter into the best three-year period in their history. They had a franchise quarterback for a while now, and more was needed to put them over the top. Shanahan had built his running game as he told Elway he would. And he built that running game around T.D. "We stumbled into Terrell," Elam said, referring to Davis' sixth-round selection. "But there was an effort there to have that caliber of a running back. We just didn't realize he was going to be the one."

When did Elway realize Davis was special? "That first year when he started feeling comfortable and getting some confidence with it and realizing that he wanted to play football," Elway said. "As good as he was, you look back at him almost leaving Tokyo on his own. He was not a huge fan of football at the time. But he got through that, and it was amazing. He was a hell of a player. He was a workhorse. We ran the (bleep) out of him."

CHAPTER EIGHT

ROD AND EDDIE MAC

When Denver Broncos owner Pat Bowlen hired Mike Shanahan as head coach in 1995, he got a two-for-one deal, as Gary Kubiak decided to come along as an offensive coordinator.

Make that a three-for-one acquisition. Wide receiver Ed McCaffrey followed Shanahan, too. "Just finished playing with the 49ers," McCaffrey said in October 2023. "We had won Super Bowl XXIX. Coach Shanahan had jumped to Denver, Coach Kubiak and a bunch of assistants joined him in Denver, and I was recruited, if you will, as a free agent to play for the Broncos."

A case can be made McCaffrey is one of the most fascinating and successful figures in sports history. At first glance, that may sound like an overstatement. But impressive as he is, we're not just talking about McCaffrey himself. We're talking about Team McCaffrey, of which there may be no peer.

Although an underrated exceptional player who may have blocked better than he caught—and his hands were good for 101 receptions one season and 1,000 yards in three—McCaffrey did not attain the superstar status of say, a Michael Jordan in basketball, Tiger Woods in golf, or John Elway in football. Yet,

McCaffrey and his families were and are second to none. It's all in the genes. Start with his nuclear family led by his dad, Edward, and mom, Elizabeth McCaffrey. Devout Catholics, Edward and Elizabeth raised five children, and Ed was the oldest. While living in Wilmington, North Carolina, Ed would play pickup basketball at Empie Park, which was where Jordan wagged his tongue during pickup games in his youth.

Edward's job later moved his family to Allentown, Pennsylvania, where son Ed's high school—strange but true—won two state basketball championships while his football team went 0–11 his junior year and 2–9 his senior year. Yet, Ed was selected to the 1985 *Parade* All-American high school football team as a 6'5", 238-pound tight end. So Ed himself was no athletic slouch. Yet, his siblings helped ratchet his status up a level. Ed's sister, Monica, was a four-year basketball player at Georgetown (1988–91). His brother Bill played for Duke, where he was the Blue Devils' second-leading scoring on their national championship team that upset UNLV in the 1991 Final Four and went on to defeat Kansas in the championship game. Bill then transferred to Vanderbilt and became the co-SEC Player of the Year with Kentucky's Jamal Mashburn in 1993. Mike McCaffrey was a four-year basketball starter at NAIA Hasson College.

Then there was Ed's married family. Wife Lisa, whom Ed met in college, was a Stanford soccer player who was also a four-year tennis letter winner in high school. Lisa's father, Dr. David Sime, played baseball, football, and track at Duke and was a 1960 Olympic silver-medal sprinter who for a time in the mid- to late-1950s was considered the World's Fastest Man.

Ed and Lisa had four sons, and all of them became standout high school and college football players. Christian McCaffrey not only made it to the next level, but he has arguably been the NFL's best running back off and on for the last five years. The youngest son, Luke McCaffrey, a quarterback in his first three college seasons at Nebraska and Rice, transitioned to receiver and averaged 64.5 catches, 857.5 yards, and nine touchdowns in 12 games a season during his junior and senior years.

Brothers, sisters, and kids all looked up to Ed. He went to Stanford to play receiver for head coach Jack Elway. A third-round draft pick of the New York Giants in 1991, McCaffrey eventually had his playing time reduced after former Broncos receiver Mark Jackson followed coach Dan Reeves from Denver in 1992. A free agent in the summer of 1994, McCaffrey turned down a couple more lucrative offers to sign with the San Francisco 49ers for the $162,000 minimum, even though he knew he would be no better than a No. 3 receiver behind Jerry Rice and John Taylor. Why? Reason No. 2 was a return to the Bay Area where he played his college ball. Reason No. 1 was McCaffrey wanted to win a Super Bowl and the 49ers, coming off back-to-back NFC Championship Game appearances, had a better chance than most.

McCaffrey registered just 11 catches for 131 yards and two touchdowns in his lone season for the 49ers. (Rice was sensational with 112 catches for 1,499 yards and 13 touchdowns.) But McCaffrey won a Super Bowl ring.

And then, as a free agent again, McCaffrey signed with the Broncos. "First and foremost, I really believed in Coach Shanahan," McCaffrey said, "because I had just got done playing a season with him and that 49ers team was one of the best teams I've ever played for right there with the Broncos' two Super Bowl teams, XXXII and XXXIII. Steve Young won Offensive Player of the Year, Deion Sanders won Defensive Player of the Year, we had 14 All-Pros, and we blew out the Chargers in the Super Bowl. So I watched the magic firsthand and saw what kind of a coach Mike Shanahan was and also Gary Kubiak, which made me want to play for those guys. But I also played for Jack Elway, John's dad, in college. He was the main reason I went to Stanford from Allentown, Pennsylvania. I had met John. He was a few years older than I was, but I met him at a breakfast one time when we were in town playing [the University of Colorado]. I remember thinking the world of him as a quarterback.

"John was pretty recognized already at that time. I thought it would be absolutely amazing to be able to play with him. So it was a little bit of everything. I was concerned at the time of the team's ability to have the kind of success we had in San Francisco because we had played the Broncos [in 1994] and beat them pretty handily during the regular season. One of my goals in life was always to be on a Super Bowl championship football team. That's one of the reasons I signed with San Francisco for significantly less than what I could have made at other places. We went on to win a Super Bowl, and it's pretty addicting. So when I was trying to decide whether this team would have the ability to win a Super Bowl, I thought with Coach Shanahan and John, I really believed we could win a Super Bowl. I believe in people. I believe it's hard to win without the right coach. It's really hard to win without the right quarterback. And Mike Shanahan was the right coach, and John Elway was the right quarterback."

For his first season with the Broncos in 1995, McCaffrey was again the No. 3 receiver. Or second teamer. His second-team receiver partner was Rod Smith, who was in his first season playing for the varsity. The Broncos' starting receivers that year were Anthony Miller and Mike Pritchard.

Smith hailed from Texarkana, Texas, where growing up he, his mom, and four siblings subsisted on government aid. He attended Division II Missouri Southern on scholarship as a quarterback. But after watching from the sidelines as a freshman, Smith received a medical redshirt in 1989 because of a torn arch in his foot. In his sophomore year of 1990, he split time between quarterback and receiver. As a junior in 1991, Smith became a full-time receiver, and the position changed his life. He led the nation with 1,439 receiving yards off 60 catches. He tore his ACL early in the third game of his senior year and received a hardship exemption. So he returned for his second senior year—sixth year in all—at Missouri Southern and became a Harlon Hill finalist (the Heisman Trophy of Division II) by compiling 63 catches for 986 yards and 13 touchdowns.

Six years of college helped Smith finish up three degrees—economics and finance, general business, and marketing and management. You can't earn that many degrees without attending class, and throughout his life, Smith was known for his attendance. He often had perfect attendance during the Broncos' offseason programs.

Despite his small-college accomplishments, Smith was not among the 222 players selected in the seven-round, 1994 NFL Draft. Perhaps he was shunned because he played against small-college competition and entered pro ball at the relatively advanced age of 24 years old. These days because of the lost COVID season, it's not unusual for pro prospects to spend five or six years in college. The advent of players getting paid through name, image, and likeness (NIL) is also enticing players, who ordinarily would jump after their redshirt sophomore or true junior seasons, to stay back for another year of college. But it the 1990s, six college years was rare for an incoming pro athlete.

Smith signed with the Broncos as an undrafted free agent in 1994 and spent his entire rookie season on the practice squad. So it took a while for such successful football men like head coach Wade Phillips, offensive coordinator Jim Fassel, and receivers coach Mo Forte to grasp what they had in Smith. What they had was a player, who despite the late start to his career, finished with team records in receptions (849), yards (11,389), and touchdown receptions (68). All those records still stand nearly 20 years after Smith played his last game. "I never felt slighted in my career at all," Smith said. "When you look at today's athletes, they looked at it where they want to be so far ahead [that] they don't live in the present. They don't accept what's right there in front of them. And for me I may have peeked at the future because I did have goals and dreams, and pro football was one of those things. But when it came across the desk, so to speak, that's what you want, but you know it's going to be hard. You know it's going to be strenuous, you know you're going to be in pain, you know you're going to cry, and it's going to hurt. That's to get your foot in the door. I'm not even talking about playing.

I knew by coming from a smaller school and the injuries I had there—but the injuries weren't the issue because it's about the heart—the heart is beating, and I put my heart into it and said I'm going to do this until I can't do it anymore, and that's what I did. I don't have any regrets."

In 1995 after the coaching change to Shanahan, Kubiak, and receivers coach Mike Heimerdinger, Smith still had to prove himself again and again before he got a chance as a starting NFL receiver. He began by playing exceptionally well on special teams. He played in all 16 games for the Broncos but had just one start at receiver. He had six tackles and a forced fumble while covering punts and kicks.

And he blocked well. That's how he eventually got playing time. "Absolutely. Here's the thing: blocking is about will," Smith said. "Technique is a portion of it, but it's more will. Like I said, I loved playing football and, when I was on the field, I played with one gear. I didn't have five gears. I didn't have a playoff gear vs. my regular-season gear. I got one gear. Earlier in my career, I would spell Anthony Miller and run a go route when I knew the ball wasn't coming. I'd run a post route, I know it's not coming. Just let me get on film. And so when it came to blocking…Ed and I made a deal—because we were both backups—we wanted to get pancake blocks. The one, who won at the end of the year, is the one who had the most pancake blocks. We knew we weren't going to get many passes, but we knew what our role was. Most of the other guys in our receiving corps didn't even know we were doing that. But that's the role we had, and we took advantage of it."

Even after he made a spectacular, walk-off, 43-yard touchdown for his first NFL catch—a contested grab in which he blocked out future Hall of Fame cornerback Darrell Green—to give the Broncos a 38–31 victory in Week Three of the 1995 season, Smith only got five more receptions the rest of the season. "I tell my friends: after my first catch, everybody was calling, my phone's blowing up. Game-winning touchdown, it's my first catch, and it's from John Elway, the whole story," Smith said. "And I didn't get a ball the next [nine] weeks after that. There weren't any fans there for the second catch."

Despite their limited playing time in 1995, Smith and McCaffrey made strong impressions on Shanahan that would lead to great years ahead. To this day, McCaffrey and Smith are the best blocking receivers in Broncos history, and perhaps only Pittsburgh Steelers wide receiver Hines Ward rivaled them among the all-time best blockers at that position in the modern-era NFL game. "Mike believed the receivers set the tone in the run game," McCaffrey said. "The linemen, the fullback, and the tight ends in the run game, they're expected to block. But for Coach Shanahan, blocking from the receivers was imperative. And there were receivers that will go unnamed who were cut because they wouldn't block in the run game, who were cut because they wouldn't finish 40 yards downfield after a catch. There were certain standards that Coach Shanahan had, and the culture that he had required the receivers to do certain things, including working hard in the run game. Rod and I used to have little side bets on who could have the most de-cleaters in a game. We had a couple guys starting ahead of us so we figured let's make this fun. Let's go knock someone on their butt. And that's the way we got noticed on film. That lasted for maybe one year. By the next year, we were playing more, and by the third year, we were starters for the rest of our careers there. Some of the most fun moments I had as a player was watching T.D., or Shannon, or Rod, or one of my teammates run past me after making a successful block. It was an incredible feeling."

Even though McCaffrey grew up around athletic prowess within his own family and had already enjoyed a good measure of his own success at both Stanford (61 catches, 917 yards, eight touchdowns in just 11 games for Dennis Green in 1990) and the NFL (team-leading 49 catches, 610 yards, five touchdowns for Ray Handley's Giants in 1992), he was a bit intimidated like everyone else when he first came across Elway as his new teammate.

An early drop frightened him, though Elway's reaction to it relaxed him. "I had already watched him on film and knew what he could do as a quarterback," McCaffrey said. "I knew he had a rocket arm. I knew he was a mobile quarterback. But until you actually play on the field with somebody, you don't know what they're really like as a teammate, as a leader. I remember the first camp I was in with John, I dropped a pass on a slant route. And immediately I thought, *Oh my gosh, how is he going to react? Is he going to tell the coach to take me out? Is he going to yell at me?* I had just got here. I didn't know how he was going to react. I admit I went into a little bit of a mini-panic mode. And he ran up to me and patted me on the back and said, 'Don't worry about it. I'll throw it right back to you.' We lined up in the huddle, called the same play, and threw it right back to me. Thank the Lord, I caught it. But to me early with the Broncos, that sent the message this guy was the real deal. He's not just incredibly talented, but he's a leader, he's a great teammate, he makes those around him better. He believes in the guys in the locker room. John always had this feeling of confidence. He always had this wry smile. He had a great sense of humor. And the guys around him felt like he was one of the guys. Even though he was kind of NFL royalty, he didn't portray himself that way. He was one of the guys in the huddle and a guy that you wanted to go to battle with, a guy you believed in."

After the 1995 season, the Broncos released Pritchard, their No. 2 receiver, ostensibly for salary cap reasons but also because Shanahan wanted to do away with the Broncos' decades-long grouping of 5'11" receivers. The Three Amigos—Vance Johnson (5'11"), Jackson (5'9") and Ricky Nattiel (5'9")—were smaller receivers. Miller and Pritchard were both 5'11" receivers. The 6'5" McCaffrey and 6'0" Smith each moved up a spot in 1996. McCaffrey became the No. 2 receiver to Miller while Smith was the No. 3 or 4 receiver with Mike Sherrard. "Eddie was a big-ass target," Elway said. "I wasn't used to big targets. We had the Three Amigos. Anthony Miller was bigger than the Three Amigos but not much. So I never really had any size at receiver. That's why it was great to add Eddie, a big, physical target. And he was huge in the running game, the way he blocked, and that's why those two—Rod and Eddie—were so good because they were so good in the running game."

After the 1996 season, Miller also was released supposedly for salary cap reasons. But the real reason why Shanahan let his top receiver Miller go was because he felt Smith was ready for a starting role. McCaffrey and Smith or Smith and McCaffrey became the Broncos' 1-2 receiving duo (along with tight end Shannon Sharpe) in the six-year period from 1997 to 2002. As the Broncos headed into their 1996 season, they had Elway as their Hall of Fame quarterback, Terrell Davis as their Hall of Fame running back, Sharpe as their Hall of Fame tight end, and McCaffrey and Smith making their moves up the depth chart at receiver.

CHAPTER NINE

THE JAW-DROPPING JAGUARS LOSS

A three-peat would have officially made John Elway's 1996–98 Denver Broncos the greatest team of the Super Bowl era. Nine teams have won back-to-back Super Bowls. No team has ever won three Super Bowls in a row.

The nine teams (with their quarterbacks) who won two Super Bowls in a row are:

1966–67 Green Bay Packers (Bart Starr)

1972–73 Miami Dolphins (Bob Griese)

1974–75 Pittsburgh Steelers (Terry Bradshaw)

1978–79 Steelers (Bradshaw)

1988–89 San Francisco 49ers (Joe Montana)

1992–93 Dallas Cowboys (Troy Aikman)

1997–98 Broncos (Elway)

2003–04 New England Patriots (Tom Brady)

2022–23 Kansas City Chiefs (Patrick Mahomes)

The Broncos missed a great chance at history at the beginning of their late-1990s run by shockingly losing to a second-year expansion team in the second round of the 1996 playoffs.

"We were as good in '96 as we were in '97 and '98," Broncos head coach Mike Shanahan said nearly 30 years later. "We should have three-peated."

In the discussion for the most heartbreaking, gut-wrenching, eyes-welling, throw-the-beer-bottle-at-the-wall, soul-bruising defeats in Broncos history, there are but two to choose from: the Jacksonville Jaguars loss in the second round of the 1996 playoffs and the Flacco Fling in the second round of the 2012 playoffs.

Elway was intimately involved in both. He was the starting quarterback, who played well, in the demoralizing defeat to the Jaguars to end the 1996 season. And he was the general manager who built a Broncos' juggernaut that lost to the Baltimore Ravens on a fluke throw to cap the 2012 season. Both upset defeats were at home in front of a sold-out Mile High crowd.

So which of those two losses was the most difficult? "Jacksonville," Elway said.

He didn't pause. His decision was made quickly.

Elway then thought back to that game. "They were a second-year expansion team," Elway said. "We had such a saga with Super Bowls. We had a great team that year, and I was getting close to the end. I mean, I wasn't close to retiring at that time, but I had more years behind me than ahead of me. You never know how many more chances you're going to have. I think that game changed Mike's mentality because that '98 year we finished against Seattle and we played the whole game."

Nearly 30 years after the No. 1-seeded Broncos' 30–27 loss to Jacksonville, Shanahan—with the perspective of time and the satisfaction of following up that terrible defeat with back-to-back Super Bowl titles during the subsequent two seasons—blamed himself for the loss. He reflected while seated at a dinner-set, white tableclothed table at his steakhouse restaurant in the Denver Tech Center on a cool, sunny mid-October afternoon in 2023. "We should have three-peated," Shanahan said. "That's why I was so ticked off at myself. I let us get away from running the ball. T.D. ran for 6.5 yards a carry and only carried the ball 14 times. But in the third quarter, Jacksonville beat us at our own game. They ran the ball right down our throat. And they threw the ball well, too. But the next time we played, we carried 49 times and we had 300 yards and five touchdowns."

The Broncos were so good in 1996 that the Jaguars were 14-point underdogs. The Broncos were almost too good. They were up 31–0 at halftime against the New York Jets in the season opener, then cruised to an easy victory. When Elway threw for two touchdowns and ran for another in a

34–7 thumping of the Seattle Seahawks on December 1, the Broncos were 12–1 and had already clinched the No. 1 AFC playoff seed with three games left in the regular season.

Staying sharp was Shanahan's only concern. In just two seasons, Shanahan had completely transformed the Broncos from a 7–9 disappointment that missed the playoffs in 1994 to the top team in the AFC. The shrewd sixth-round selection of Terrell Davis was a major addition, yes, but T.D.'s impact overshadowed the fact the Broncos' resurrection primarily came about because of a rebuilt defense. In 1994, the year before Shanahan arrived, the Broncos ranked last among the 28 NFL teams in total defense. They improved to 15th among 30 teams in Shanahan's first season in 1995, though they still ranked 23rd against the rush. In 1996 the Broncos ranked first against the rush and fourth overall in team defense.

Offensively, the improvement wasn't nearly as dramatic; the notable exceptions were Davis and the running game. The Broncos ranked sixth in total offense in 1994 and No. 1 in 1996. The difference was made up in the running game, where the Broncos improved from 23rd in 1994 to first in 1996.

Among the 55 players on the Broncos' 1996 roster, only 20 remained from the Dan Reeves/Wade Phillips era. Since Shanahan took control two years before, 18 of the 35 new players were on defense, including eight of the 11 starters. The offense still had six pre-Shanahan starters. "I was hoping that he would do what he did," free safety Steve Atwater, the senior member of the defense told the *Colorado Springs Gazette-Telegraph*. "It just shows he's the kind of person who's focused and he knows what our weaknesses were."

Atwater said new personnel weren't the only reason why the Broncos were considered to have an NFC-type defense. Since Shanahan and defensive coordinator Greg Robinson took control, the Broncos' front four lined up closer together, and the secondary played less zone. NFC teams had won 12 Super Bowls in a row in part because the NFC was the more physical of the two conferences. Shanahan set out to emulate that physicality by making sweeping personnel changes on defense, especially in the box area where he brought in Alfred Williams, Michael Dean Perry, and Mike Lodish to fortify the defensive line. At linebacker John Mobley was a first-round rookie starter along with veteran Bill Romanowski, who had two Super Bowl rings from his 49ers years.

Despite the Broncos' improvements on defense, the Packers would extend the NFC streak to 13 straight Super Bowls after winning Super Bowl XXXI to cap the 1996 season. Denver stumbled at the end of its season, including when it faced the Packers. It's impossible to get a team to play at peak performance when it has nothing to play for. In Denver's 14th game, Shanahan rested Elway, who had an aching left hamstring, and started Bill Musgrave at quarterback against the Packers, the top team in the NFC, at Lambeau Field. Most, but not all, of the other starters played, but clearly the Broncos hearts and souls weren't in it. The Packers destroyed the Broncos 41–6.

The Broncos could never recapture their edge. Even though they led the NFL in rushing thanks to Davis with 147.6 yards per game, the Broncos finished with three consecutive subpar rushing performances against Green Bay (93 yards), the Oakland Raiders (99 yards), and the San Diego Chargers (66 yards). It was a tell to how the season would despondently finish.

Elway had one of his best seasons to finish with 3,328 passing yards and 26 touchdown passes to tie his career high. He finished second to Green Bay's Brett Favre in MVP voting and was headed to his seventh Pro Bowl. But in the final three games, he sat out one and played only the first quarter in the season finale, a 16–10 loss to the Chargers. Besides coasting through their final three games without much zest, the Broncos had a first-round playoff bye. More inertia. The finely-tuned machine had sat idle in the garage for too long by the time they hosted Jacksonville on January 4, 1997 at Mile High Stadium.

Still, it was only the Jaguars. Or as Woody Paige called them in *The Denver Post* sports column on the morning of the game, the "Jagwads." The Paige column so degraded the upstart Jacksonville franchise that it was all anyone was talking about in the hours leading up to the game. Some excerpts from the piece:

> Jacksonville Jagwads? What league are they in?
>
> When did the NFL start letting USFL teams participate in the playoffs? Did I miss something? Or, are the Jags from that goofy World League or the Continental Basketball Association?
>
> How do you get worked up to play somebody called Jacksonville with a bunch of nobodies? Who wants to hurl insults and snowballs at Jagwads?
>
> The Broncos go 13–3, yet are forced by the league to play kissyface with Jagwads. Bring on Pittsburgh—a mean team with meat on the bone.
>
> Wasn't Jackson (Miss.) State available?
>
> Denver–Jacksonville will be known as "The Blowout." The Broncos are favored by 14. Not enough.
>
> Broncos 31, Jags 10.
>
> Can we get a legitimate NFL team in here next Sunday?

Afterward, when the Jaguars pulled off the upset, Tony Boselli, the Jaguars' eventual Hall of Fame left tackle who grew up in Boulder, Colorado, was sitting in a chair in front of his locker, wearing a wide grin. "That Woody Paige article?" Boselli said. "Tell him he did us a favor."

After the game Paige quoted Jaguars coach Tom Coughlin as saying he wanted to thank the columnist. "He did a nice job this morning...I mean, that was an out-and-out flagrant violation of respect. There's no call for that."

After the Broncos' stunning loss, Paige also wrote: "This was the most unsettling and upsetting defeat in Colorado sports history and the most startling upset in the NFL since the New York Jets confounded the Baltimore Colts in Super Bowl III."

Nearly 30 years later, Elway didn't remember so much that his team was flat or rusty against the Jaguars. Immediately after that game and again with 27 years gone by, Elway gave credit where credit was due. "They played well. I know Brunell played well," Elway said in November 2023. "That was a heartbreaker. You have home-field advantage, 13–3. That happened to us one other time. I think it was '84. We lost to Pittsburgh. I think we had home field that year, too. We were 13–3. That Jacksonville loss, though, was devastating because of the year we'd had, and I know I'm getting older, thought we had a shot. The fact we had a good team probably made that the hardest loss."

Broncos owner Pat Bowlen noted the similarities between the loss to Jacksonville in 1996 and to Pittsburgh in 1984. "Long time off before a meaningful game," he told the *Rocky*

Mountain News. "A week in between before the first playoff game, a shoo-in, a large favorite to win."

But 1984 was his first year as Broncos owner, and again that team was Elway-centric. With a dozen more years of NFL ownership experience, Bowlen knew the 1996 Broncos were a more complete team. "I've said all year that, 'this is the best team I've ever been associated with,'" Bowlen said. "I still believe that. We just had a meltdown at a time when we didn't have to. This is a game we should have won...I think this is a lesson for us. We'll learn something by this. We won't forget this for a long, long time."

Shannon Sharpe, to no one's surprise, was the most expressive in response to the Broncos' heartbreak. "I just want to cry," Sharpe said. "I want to go home, sit on that couch and cry. I don't want to hear, 'Hey, you guys had a great season,' or 'There's always next year.' I don't want to hear it."

Left guard Mark Schlereth was more philosophical about the stunning loss. He didn't feel it coming exactly or at least he didn't want to admit it, as those bad feelings were infiltrating his soul. But he was concerned following a practice leading up to the game. "More than the rest, it was really game planning more than anything else," Schlereth said. "I think Mike would tell you the same thing. We were a dominant run football team, and I think Terrell got 12 carries for 95 yards or something like that."

Spoken like a true offensive lineman from the 1990s. It was actually 14 carries and 91 yards for Davis against Jacksonville. "The way we ran our offense that week, we ran this check-with-me system, and I remember I came home Wednesday after practice, and my wife, who's astute, said, 'What's wrong?'" Schlereth recalled in October 2023. "I said, 'I don't like what we're doing.' Probably the only time I came home where I was, 'I don't like what we're doing.' She was, 'What do you mean?' It was almost like the coaches wanted to be perfect. And sometimes—and this happens in today's day and age a lot—you want to be perfect on everything and you know you want a premium play against everything. That's one of the terms that coaches use. Sometimes you need to just call it and run it and be tougher than the other team and not have to think, not just react. For us our offense that week was if they're going to give us certain looks, we're going to check out and throw the ball. And so they gave us a bunch of looks, which limited Terrell to [14] carries, which was ridiculous. *You're averaging 6.5 yards per carry. You're kicking the (bleep) out of them and you only give it to him 14 times?* That's where we usually give it to Terrell 25 times. It's one of those things where you live and learn. It was a hard lesson, but that was the catalytic event that led us to back-to-back championships. So I can't complain too much. It was a hard lesson and the most painful loss of my career, but at the same time, it did spur us on to back-to-back world championships."

In fairness to Shanahan, Davis suffered a knee injury in the second quarter that knocked him out a few plays and rendered him less effective than the 1,538-yard runner he was during the regular season. Davis had 56 yards rushing in the first quarter as the Broncos built a 12–0 lead. He had 35 rushing yards the rest of the game as the Jaguars ran off a 30–20 advantage before Elway directed a late touchdown drive. "It was a tough game," said receiver Ed McCaffrey, who caught a 15-yard touchdown pass with 1:50 remaining to draw the Broncos within 30–27. "Brunell was very slippery, and they made some plays offensively. I remember us fighting back. We caught a touchdown late in the game and we didn't get the onside kick, but we competed till the bitter end. It wasn't our day. They played better than we did on that day, which was a shocker because we feel we were just as good that year as we were the next year. But it goes to show you how hard it is to win a Super Bowl. You have one bad day as a team and you don't win a Super Bowl."

But something happened the next day that gave McCaffrey hope the sky wasn't falling. McCaffrey knows about how bad the next day can be. In the Broncos' new stadium-opening game on Monday night, September 10, 2001, McCaffrey suffered a gruesome compound fracture in his leg. The injury happened in front of a primetime, national audience. Shortly after midnight on September 11, McCaffrey underwent surgery to repair the leg. He was lying in a hospital room with a morphine drip as he watched on television the second tower get hit on 9/11. "It was a bad day," McCaffrey has said. "And an even worse tomorrow."

Twenty-two years later, McCaffrey remembers how his team first started to bounce back from the Jacksonville defeat. "I remember we had resolve," he said. "I remember how upset my teammates were after the game. Guys were in tears. I also remember the next day that guys were cleaning out their lockers and could leave if they wanted. The season's over, but three quarters of the team was lifting. It was almost like they didn't get the message. The season's over yet guys were still in there lifting weights. I remember Gary Kubiak leaned over to me and said, 'Hey, check this out.'"

McCaffrey was lifting weights, but his mind was elsewhere. On the game that got away. On the season that got away. "[I] wasn't even paying attention," McCaffrey said. "And [Kubiak] said, 'Look at how many guys are in here working out. These guys can be on a plane right now.' He goes, 'This is how I know we're going to be great.' He said that in the weight room the day after that loss. And then we go on to win two more Super Bowls. Once he pointed it out to me, I realized we've got the right guys on this team. These guys are going to stay committed, stay connected, and work hard to be even better."

Looking back, some Broncos have a tinge of regret their 1996 team didn't join their 1997–98 championships for a three-peat. Davis more than anyone, though, says 1997 and 1998 may not have happened if not for the bitter defeat to Jacksonville in 1996. "The Jacksonville loss was everything you could imagine," Davis said. "I don't know if gut-punch is able to describe it. It ripped everything that we had worked for. It was so unbelievable. I remember I was sitting with Shannon [Sharpe] after the game. They probably had to come get us off the bench after because I couldn't believe the game was over. I kept looking up at the scoreboard thinking, *Come on. There's got to be another quarter. This can't be real. This must be a joke.* I mean, it hurt. It hurt. But after that to capture that emotion and that hole that was in my chest, it was good to remember that because I never wanted that feeling again. I know I made a commitment to myself and I know everybody made the commitment that we don't ever want to experience that feeling again. I think '96 helped us out. I think most people on our team look at '96 as if we didn't lose that game to Jacksonville, I don't know if we would have had the same drive or hunger."

Elway agreed. "There's no doubt it helped us win the next two," Elway said. "Especially the next year."

Said Schlereth: "I agree totally with T.D. I think the other thing is: I know we would have gone to the Super Bowl that year because New England—we used to beat New England like a drum. That was a given. But I don't know how that Green Bay game would have gone."

Maybe the Broncos weren't ready to beat Green Bay in the ultimate game in 1996. Maybe they were. We'll never know. What we do know is they were ready for Brett Favre and the Packers when it counted in 1997.

CHAPTER TEN

1997'S NEW LOOK, FRESH ATTITUDE

With the context of time, the new uniforms the Denver Broncos broke out starting with the 1997 season marked the greatest fashion upgrade in the history of sports. In the first 37 seasons of the Denver franchise, it had used three different logos, four helmet designs, and five uniform ensembles. None of the looks brought the Broncos' owner and star players to the Super Bowl stage to accept the Lombardi Trophy.

Then in February 1997, the Broncos dropped their traditional orange color in favor of navy blue, added thick Nike swoosh stripes, erased the "D" and bucking Bronco from their logo, replaced it with a leaner, meaner Bronco, and voila! The Broncos won back-to-back Super Bowls in their first two seasons with the new uniforms, color schemes, and logo. When a team wins two Super Bowls in the first two years of their uniform style, it wouldn't matter if the gameday dress clashed polka dotted jerseys with striped pants. That's a good uniform.

The home, navy blue jerseys would stay until 2012 when for the first season of the Peyton Manning-era the primary home uniforms returned to the orange tops, white bottoms, and orange/white shoes while keeping the same logo and dark-blue helmet. The road jerseys since 1997 have been white with navy blue striping.

Not that the new uniforms were popular when Broncos owner Pat Bowlen revealed the new look during a February 1997 press conference. Its detractors included this author who wrote this in his *Colorado Springs Gazette-Telegraph* column: "The Broncos don't have new home uniforms; owner Pat Bowlen had someone steal them from the Chicago Bears' equipment room. It's not so much that the Broncos' new uniform design is repulsive. It lacks creativity. After 29 years of Orange Crush, Bowlen wants the Broncos to become the Monsters of Midway."

This review would have softened considerably with time—and the accumulation of the ultimate hardware. When the Broncos started the 1997 season 6–0 and 9–2, the new No. 7 and No. 30 navy blue jerseys flew off the racks at sporting goods, discount department, and grocery stores.

The team's start was remarkable, considering the numerous unique challenges greeting the Broncos' season. Top receiver Anthony Miller was released for financial reasons but also because head coach Mike Shanahan wanted more of the unselfish Ed McCaffrey and Rod Smith to lead his receiver room. More troubling was that the Broncos' best offensive lineman, left tackle Gary Zimmerman, retired after the 1996 season because his shoulder was so beat up he didn't think he could throw one more block. Late in the season, Shanahan released disgruntled star defensive tackle Michael Dean Perry with one regular-season week remaining on his then-handsome contract of three years and $7.2 million.

There was also the potential damaging psyche of the team that twice required Shanahan's coaching genius. The first was getting over the Jacksonville Jaguars loss. To have climbed the mountaintop so quickly during the regular season—the No. 1 AFC playoff seed was clinched with three games remaining— only to come crashing down in a matter of three hours by one of the best games the Jaguars have played in their 30-year history—was devastating.

Shanahan was able to galvanize his team, though, by making sure each one of his top players knew they would be the difference between another run at the Super Bowl or a season of excuse-making disappointment. Not him. Not Bowlen. The players. He wanted the players to take ownership of the team. They were a mature enough group to embrace the challenge. "The chemistry from the core guys, we were really tight," kicker Jason Elam recalled. "We bonded really well. We never wanted to let anybody down. That's not always the case. You never know how teams are going to bond and how the chemistry is going to be. So Mike did a really good job of creating an environment where we really did work well together."

The key to the team's attitude was John Elway. One of the more underrated characteristics of leadership is obedience. If the star player rolls his eyes at the head coach's speech to the team and only half-heartedly carries out the boss' demands, then the other players will roll their eyes and go through the motions. If the star quarterback is two minutes late to a meeting, why would the others show up five minutes early? But when Elway demonstrated determination through his conditioning, training in the weight room, and commitment to offseason practice, the rest of the team busted their butts with sweat, strain, and detailed workouts. "I've learned that John's mood is always a good barometer for how this team will fare," Bowlen told the *Rocky Mountain News* prior to the 1997 season. "John always works hard in the offseason relative to the other players, but his intensity and his enthusiasm this offseason was as good as I've ever seen it."

Terrell Davis, the Broncos' young star running back who had surpassed 1,100 and 1,500 yards rushing in his first two seasons, led the narrative 25 years later that Denver's back-to-back Super Bowl titles in 1997–98 does not happen without the disappointment of Jacksonville. "Every time we were practicing or things weren't going well, man to man it was, 'Hey, man, Jacksonville,'" Davis said in November 2023. "That was our immediate response. So we are able to use that big time every time we felt like there was slippage or a point where we weren't focused. And even when we were about to play a team we were supposed to dominate, we had to remind ourself, 'Jacksonville.'"

Without Elway as the primary leader in the locker room, without the special core of leaders, without Shanahan's innate ability to read the room and address its elephant, the Broncos would not have been able to overcome the potentially divisive, late-season incident involving the team's linebacker Bill Romanowski, who was caught by *Monday Night Football* cameras spitting in the face of San Francisco 49ers receiver J.J. Stokes. When a couple days later, Broncos tight end Shannon Sharpe and receiver Willie Green ripped Romanowski for his overt disrespectful act toward Stokes, the fear was the team would become racially divided. The loss to San Francisco was the Broncos' third in four games, and there was one more game left in the regular season. The mood in the locker room was somber enough. The Romo incident could have sparked in-house dissension.

But after Shanahan called a team meeting the Thursday before the regular-season finale against the San Diego Chargers, all players came away stating the same message. Romanowski profusely apologized. Sharpe and Green made sure the media understood they did not believe Romanowski was a racist or that his spitting incident was a racially motivated act. Just in time, all the Broncos were pulling on the same rope again.

Here is how the 1997 journey to the first Super Bowl title in franchise history unfolded:

Game One
August 31—Broncos 19, Kansas City Chiefs 3 at Mile High Stadium

The Denver Broncos defense held Kansas City Chiefs quarterback Elvis Grbac to just 115 yards passing and aging running back Marcus Allen (in his final season) to -2 yards rushing on three carries and no receptions. There was concern as to whether John Elway would be able to play the season opener after he suffered torn biceps in his right throwing arm during a preseason game August 4 against the Miami Dolphins in Mexico City. In that same American Bowl preseason exhibition, Denver defensive end Alfred Williams, who led the team with 13 sacks the previous year, suffered a torn triceps.

But less than four weeks later, Elway played well in Game One, throwing for 246 yards on 17-of-28 passing. Terrell Davis rushed for 101 tough yards as it came off 26 carries. The game raised concern about the Broncos' offensive tackle positions as Tony Jones and Jamie Brown initially seemed a step down from predecessors Gary Zimmerman and Broderick Thompson.

The sellout crowd held its breath late in the first half as the battered Elway tried to catch his after taking a rib shot from Chiefs safety Jerome Woods, who was a split-second late in delivering what appeared to be an intentional blow with his elbow. Elway had delivered a long, arching pass to Rod Smith for a 78-yard gain to the Chiefs' 8, setting up Jason Elam's third field goal for a 9–0 halftime lead. "But I didn't care about the catch," Elway said at his postgame press conference. "I just wanted to breathe again."

Woods was later fined by the league for his hit.

Game Two
September 7—Broncos 35, Seattle Seahawks 14 at the Kingdome

That torn biceps tendon? After two games John Elway was 35-of-54 (64.8 percent) for 443 yards, two touchdowns, and no interceptions. He threw two touchdown passes to Ed McCaffrey in this one. Terrell Davis had another 107 yards on 21 carries, and Darrien Gordon highlighted another strong defensive effort with a 32-yard, pick-six off Warren Moon.

Game Three
September 14—Broncos 35, St. Louis Rams 14 at Mile High Stadium

The story leading into the game was the return of Gary Zimmerman. The left tackle ended his retirement during the week, practicing for the first time the Wednesday before the game. He was only supposed to play 25 to 30 snaps, but when tackle Tony Jones hurt an ankle, Zimmerman wound up playing almost the entire game. His impact was immediate. John Elway suddenly had time to throw again. "Zim played really well," Elway said. "I didn't get any pressure from that side."

Elway threw four more touchdown passes—including scoring strikes of 72 and 38 yards to Rod Smith—and for 247 more yards as the Denver Broncos picked up their second consecutive three-touchdown romp. By game's end Elway had 257 career touchdown passes, moving ahead of Dan Fouts (254) and Sonny Jurgensen (255) for sixth most in NFL history. Elway also rose to No. 2 in all-time pass attempts (6,474), jumping past Fran Tarkenton. "It's flattering to pass some of those names because those guys are some of my childhood heroes," Elway said. "But I just hope there's a lot more."

Darrien Gordon had a 94-yard punt return for a touchdown early in the second half to begin the onslaught. Terrell Davis had another workmanlike 103-yards-off-21-carry performance.

Game Four
September 21—Broncos 38, Cincinnati Bengals 20 at Mile High Stadium

Terrell Davis busted out with 215 yards rushing, including a 50-yard touchdown run in the fourth quarter that gave the

Denver Broncos a 28–20 lead. "Terrell is the best running back in the NFL," John Elway said after the game. Elway also threw three touchdown passes—two to Rod Smith and the other to McCaffrey.

Denver defensive end Alfred Williams, the most gregarious player on the team, completed a 51-yard fumble return off a Neil Smith strip-sack for a touchdown by making a swan dive into the end zone.

Game Five

September 28—Broncos 29, Atlanta Falcons 21 at Georgia Dome

Owner Pat Bowlen, who fired Dan Reeves following the 1992 season, sought out his former head coach during pregame warmups. They seemed to have a friendly conversation. Steve Atwater, Tyrone Braxton, and Shannon Sharpe also greeted their former coach, who was now the Atlanta Falcons head coach. Not greeting Reeves was John Elway, who publicly feuded with the head coach during their final three seasons together, or Mike Shanahan, whom Reeves fired as offensive coordinator following the 1991 season.

Reeves and Shanahan did meet at midfield after the game and hugged each other. The Denver Broncos jumped out to a 23–0 lead on two Elway touchdown passes—one a 65-yarder to Sharpe—and a 13-yard Terrell Davis touchdown run, plus two Davis two-point conversion runs. The Falcons made it a game, drawing within one score early in the fourth quarter, but the Broncos held on. "This was just a typical Dan Reeves game," a diplomatic Elway said afterward. "His team hung in there. That's why we always had so many comeback wins."

Elway was off to one of the best five-game starts of his career with 12 touchdown passes against just three interceptions.

Game Six

October 6—Broncos 34, New England Patriots 13 at Mile High Stadium

In this much-hyped *Monday Night Football* battle of unbeatens, the Denver Broncos whipped the New England Patriots, who were the defending AFC champions after beating Jacksonville one week after the Jaguars stunned Denver in the previous year's playoffs.

Terrell Davis rushed for 171 yards and two touchdowns. This was the game when T.D.'s Mile High Salute was adopted by the rest of his teammates. "You're always thinking about the playoffs because that's all that counts," Davis said afterward. "But we know what happened last year. We won the regular season last year, too, and look what happened."

The previous year the Patriots had lost to the Green Bay Packers in Super Bowl XXXI. "Watching New England in the Super Bowl was motivation for us tonight," Elway said.

It was the Broncos' ninth straight win against the Patriots, and the last four wins were by a combined 125–27.

Game Seven
October 19—Oakland Raiders 28, Broncos 25 at Oakland-Alameda County Coliseum

The Oakland Raiders' Napoleon Kaufman rushed for 227 yards, exposing Denver's questionable run defense. Jason Elam, the Broncos' normally superb placekicker, was bothered by a hip flexor-groin injury and missed two field goals. John Elway threw for 309 yards, including a touchdown pass to Ed McCaffrey for his only 300-yard passing game of the season. Terrell Davis rushed for two touchdowns, a two-point conversion, and 85 yards off 23 carries.

Game Eight
October 26—Broncos 23, Buffalo Bills 20 at Rich Stadium

The Blizzard Game. Not a Buffalo blizzard. Starting the Friday night before the game, the Denver area was bombarded with two-plus feet of snow. The greatest challenge about this game was getting to it. Denver Broncos players were stranded

Saturday morning while trying to drive from their homes to team headquarters where the team buses awaited. Amidst some controversy, the city and county of Denver made special snowplow maneuvers for the team buses to get through the otherwise closed Peña Boulevard road to the Denver International Airport.

The Broncos arrived in Buffalo after midnight Sunday morning—fewer than 13 hours before the 1:00 PM EST kickoff. "I really didn't think there was a chance for us to get out of there," Shanahan said after the victory. "It's a credit to the people of Denver, people lending snowmobiles and tractors and other sorts of equipment to get our players out of some areas that they normally couldn't have gotten out of. We didn't play in that snowstorm, but we had to deal with it."

In a remarkable showing of resolve and mental toughness, the Broncos—despite their fatigue—went up 20–0 with 4:13 left in the third quarter after defensive tackle Keith Traylor returned a Todd Collins interception 62 yards for a touchdown. At that point the long weekend caught up to the Broncos, who blew the 20–0 lead in the fourth quarter. The Broncos then dug deep again late in the overtime period. Elway hit back-to-back passes to Ed McCaffrey and Rod Smith for 17 and 14 yards, and Terrell Davis did the rest to set up a short field goal for Elam, who nailed the game-winner.

"That's as long of a weekend as I've ever had in my lifetime," Alfred Williams said.

The win impressed the Broncos head coach. "To handle the type of adversity that we've had for the last day and a half, to play like we did, and then to come back in overtime the way we did really says a lot about the character of this football team," Mike Shanahan said.

Incredibly, Davis carried the ball a team-record 42 times for 207 yards. It was his second 200-yard performance in five games and gave him 1,068 yards at the halfway mark of the season—a pace of 2,136 yards, which put Eric Dickerson's still-standing single-season record of 2,105 yards set in 1984 in danger. "I was thinking more about the carries than the yardage," an exhausted Davis said after the game. "It felt more like 51, 52, 53 toward the end."

Game Nine
November 2—Broncos 30, Seattle Seahawks 27 at Mile High Stadium

John Elway had a big day by throwing for 252 yards, including touchdown passes to Willie Green (10 yards) and Rod Smith (59 yards). That gave him 47,019 career passing yards to move past Fran Tarkenton (47,003) into second place on the all-time passing yardage list. Elway only trailed his 1983 draft classmate Dan Marino, who never did relinquish his career passing records until 20 years later when the likes of Brett Favre, Peyton Manning, Drew Brees, and Tom Brady went by. Elway also joined Marino and Tarkenton as the only three players to surpass 50,000 career yards of total offense. "These records mean a lot to me," Elway said. "But I feel like I've got a lot left."

Shaking off soreness from his 42-carry game the week before in Buffalo, Terrell Davis still managed to rush for 101 yards on 21 carries. Ho hum.

Game 10
November 9—Broncos 34, Carolina Panthers 0 at Mile High Stadium

The previous year the Carolina Panthers behind second-year, first-round draft pick Kerry Collins reached the NFC Championship Game as a second-year expansion team—just like the Jacksonville Jaguars. The Panthers and Denver Broncos met during the preseason when Bill Romanowski drew a then substantial $20,000 fine for his hit that broke Collins' jaw in two places. Collins missed the rest of the preseason and first two games of the regular season. He should have sat out this one. Collins completed just 13-of-29 passes for 141 yards and was intercepted three times.

The fabulous Darrien Gordon started the Broncos' rout with back-to-back punt returns for touchdowns of 82 and

75 yards in the first quarter. Ray Crockett's two interceptions and Tyrone Braxton's 27-yard touchdown interception return in the fourth quarter completed the defense's big day. Braxton's touchdown was the Broncos' ninth by the defense or special teams through 10 games.

John Elway threw for 227 yards and a touchdown without an interception, and Terrell Davis had a machine-like 104 yards on 21 carries. "The best thing about this offense," Sharpe told the *Colorado Springs Gazette-Telegraph*, "is that Terrell comes into the locker room in his street clothes with 120 rushing yards. And John Elway has 250 passing yards driving down the highway before he even gets to the stadium."

At this point, the Broncos were two games ahead of the 7–3 Kansas City Chiefs in the AFC West. As it turned out, this would be Denver's high-water mark of the regular season. The Great Colorado Blizzard was behind them, but several more obstacles loomed ahead.

Game 11

November 16—Kansas City Chiefs 24, Broncos 22 at Arrowhead Stadium

Down 21–19 with five minutes remaining, John Elway engineered one of his patented fourth-quarter comebacks, using back-to-back completions to Willie Green for 13 and 25 yards to drive the Denver Broncos from their own 24 to the Kansas City 15. Jason Elam kicked a go-ahead, 34-yard field goal right at the two-minute warning.

But Kansas City Chiefs backup quarterback Rich Gannon, who started in place of the injured Elvis Grbac, shook off a rough game by completing four passes for 41 yards in the hurry-up offense. Before then, Gannon was just 7-of-16 for 57 yards. Gannon got the Chiefs close enough for Pete Stoyanovich to boot a game-winning, 54-yard field goal as time expired.

"Some losses hurt worse than others," Shannon Sharpe said. "This one stings bad."

Terrell Davis again was heavily used on the road, carrying 34 times for 127 yards.

Game 12

November 24—Broncos 31, Oakland Raiders 3 at Mile High Stadium

Nothing like a rivalry game against the Oakland Raiders to help the Denver Broncos overcome their tough loss in Kansas City. Terrell Davis only rushed for 69 yards on 21 carries, but three went for touchdowns. Meanwhile, the Denver D focused on stopping Raiders running back Napolean Kaufman, who had just 53 yards on 13 carries—well below his 227-yard performance when the teams met five weeks earlier. "We've been thinking about this game for weeks. It's dominated our thoughts," said Alfred Williams. "I mean revenge is a sweet thing."

Shannon Sharpe had 10 catches for 142 yards, and John Elway iced the win with a 15-yard touchdown pass to Rod Smith.

Game 13

November 30—Broncos 38, San Diego Chargers 28 at Qualcomm Stadium

Before their primetime *Sunday Night Football* game kicked off, many Denver Broncos players watched on TV as the Kansas City Chiefs destroyed the San Francisco 49ers 44–9, ending San Francisco's 11-game winning streak. Marty Schottenheimer's Chiefs were on fire, as they would crush the Oakland Raiders the following week 30–0. After losing to the Jacksonville Jaguars to fall to 7–3, the Chiefs didn't lose another game in the regular season, finishing 13–3. The Broncos would only hold the Chiefs off for one more week.

They did take care of business against the San Diego Chargers in front of a national audience. Terrell Davis, who grew up in San Diego, rushed for 178 yards for his team-record 10th 100-yard game of the season. It also gave him 1,647 rushing yards, meaning he needed a doable 353 yards in his final three games to join O.J. Simpson and Eric Dickerson as the only running backs in NFL history to crack the 2,000-yard milestone.

John Elway threw for 240 yards and three touchdowns—two to Ed McCaffrey, one to Rod Smith—and safety Steve Atwater had a 22-yard touchdown interception return late in the first half to give the visiting Broncos a 28–7 lead. But this was the last time during the regular season the local media believed the Broncos had what it took to finally win their first Super Bowl. Trouble was ahead both on the field and in the locker room.

Game 14

December 7—Pittsburgh Steelers 35, Broncos 24 at Three Rivers Stadium

For the first time this season, the Denver Broncos were not leading the AFC West as the Kansas City Chiefs matched their 11–3 record and held the division record tiebreaker. With the Chiefs also having the easier remaining schedule, the local columnists were opining that without home-field advantage in the playoffs, the elusive Super Bowl championship would again not come to Denver. And the media weren't the only skeptics. "There's no question this loss hurt us," Steve Atwater said. "We'll have to see how bad. We just have to hope it won't cost us a chance to play at home in the playoffs. If it does, we might be wasting a good season."

Rod Smith had a big game, catching touchdown passes of 37 and 25 yards from John Elway to give the visiting Broncos a 21–7 lead early in the second quarter. Terrell Davis had his 21 carries but for only 75 yards, meaning he would need 278 yards in his final two games to reach 2,000. As it turned out, it was his last chance as an injury in the next game at the San Francisco 49ers would limit him to just one more half in the final two weeks.

But the Broncos couldn't hold on to their early, two-touchdown lead. Pittsburgh Steelers quarterback Kordell "Slash" Stewart was sensational, throwing for 303 yards and three touchdowns and rushing for another 49 yards and two more touchdowns. Jerome Bettis, the Steelers' 252-pound running back, rushed for 125 yards on 24 carries. If the two teams were to meet again in the playoffs at Three Rivers, there didn't seem to be much doubt that the Steelers would be favored.

Game 15

December 15—San Francisco 49ers 34, Broncos 17 at 3Com Park

The epitaphs on the Denver Broncos' season following this game were written in various forms. On so many levels, this game was a disaster, starting with Terrell Davis suffering a separated right shoulder late in the first half. That injury would end his regular season. John Elway threw two interceptions and lost a fumble that led to 17 San Francisco 49ers points. The Chiefs clinched the AFC West title, meaning the Broncos would have to go through the playoffs as a wild-card.

The most disconcerting element to this loss, though, was Bill Romanowski getting caught by the *Monday Night Football* cameras spitting in the face of 49ers receiver J.J. Stokes during the third quarter. The league announced two days later that Romanowski was fined $7,500, prompting two of his teammates, Sharpe and Willie Green, to wonder out loud if the punishment shouldn't have been stiffer. "Romo did the worst thing that he can do to a person, especially of our background and our race," Sharpe told the *Rocky Mountain News* on Wednesday, two days after the game. "I wonder what would have happened to [Black defensive players] Alfred Williams or Neil Smith had they done that to [White 49ers quarterback] Steve Young.

"I don't give a (expletive) what color you are," Green said. "It's disrespecting a man to spit in his face. That's one of the things my parents taught me. You don't spit in nobody's face."

Upon realizing his spitting incident was caught on prime-time television and was replayed countless times by ESPN programming, Romanowski apologized profusely. "What I did was totally inexcusable and I'm sorry," Romanowski said. "I was wrong in what I did. When emotion is high, logic is low."

But the comments by Sharpe and Green in the Thursday morning papers caused Shanahan to call a Thursday team meeting. "People expressed how they felt," Romanowski told the *Colorado Springs Gazette-Telegraph*. "They said to me there are no hard feelings toward me. They told me they don't agree with what I did. But I don't expect anybody in this country to agree with what I did."

Sharpe and Green told Romanowski that in no way did they mean to imply that he was a racist. "Some of this was blown out of proportion," Sharpe said. "I do not think this was a racial issue. I do not think Romo is a racist."

"This is over with as far as I'm concerned," Green said. "I said what I had to say."

The meeting worked. It had calmed the furor. "Any time things are said, you always have to talk about it," Mike Shanahan said. "I think communication's the key to problems. If you think a problem exists, then you communicate. What was said, guys were being very honest with how they felt, and everybody had their different opinions."

Had the Romo spitting incident occurred in today's atmosphere of social media and social justice, there's no telling how much it would have escalated. But in 1997 Romanowski's egregious act against Stokes did not divide the Broncos locker room. "There are two ways to take what happened,"

Romanowksi said. "Let it split the team apart or bring us together and make us that much tighter and stronger."

Game 16
December 21—Broncos 38, San Diego Chargers 3 at Mile High Stadium

It took a couple days for the spitting incident to mushroom into an uproar. Bill Romanowski's disrespectful act occurred late on Monday night, as the Denver Broncos' reporters were up against deadline. It was bad enough that the loss to the San Francisco 49ers meant the Broncos' Super Bowl hopes appeared to be dwindling as the team had lost three of four to lose the AFC West title and postseason home-field advantage to the Kansas City Chiefs.

And then Tuesday the day after the defeat to San Francisco, Shanahan made the bold move of releasing highly paid defensive tackle Michael Dean Perry. A six-time Pro Bowler and five-time All Pro with the Cleveland Browns, Perry, the younger brother of famed former Chicago Bears nose tackle William "Refrigerator" Perry, had signed a monstrous, three-year, $7.2 million deal with Denver as a free agent prior to the 1995 season.

He got in the doghouse of Broncos Country when he walked, not jogged, off the field in the 1996 season-ending, playoff loss to the Jacksonville Jaguars. That reprehensible act of laziness resulted in a 12-man-on-the-field penalty that kept a Jaguars drive alive, which resulted in a touchdown. Heading into the 1997 season, Perry believed an offseason toe surgery negatively affected his left knee. He said the Broncos' medical team recommended a cleanup procedure on his knee, but he elected to keep playing and he started the first eight games. But Shanahan wasn't happy with his production or practice habits, and Perry was inactive for five of the next six games until he received his walking papers prior to the final game against the San Diego Chargers. Shanahan sent out a statement indicating the parting of ways was mutual: "He decided that he did not wish to remain with the club unless he could be assured that he would be active and would play in the club's remaining games. The club could not give him that assurance and agreed to release him from his contract."

Perry was gone from the season finale and so was Terrell Davis, though for a very different reason. Davis had a separated shoulder and finished the season with 1,750 yards—second to Detroit Lions running back Barry Sanders who was able to accomplish his 2,000-yard quest with 2,053. But even without Davis, the Broncos accumulated 451 total yards. They still had John Elway after all. He capped his 15th regular season by throwing for four touchdowns—two to Rod Smith, one to Ed McCaffrey, and a 68-yard strike to Shannon Sharpe. The offensive line allowed no sacks and helped Derek

Loville and Vaughn Hebron combine for 113 yards rushing on 26 carries in T.D.'s place. "I think we're okay now," Sharpe said afterward.

Added linebacker Bill Romanowksi: "I can't say I have ever experienced a longer week in my career. I actually think what happened to me helped take the pressure off the guys."

The Broncos finished the regular season with the NFL's highest-scoring offense at 29.6 points per game. Their defense was sixth best by allowing just 17.9 points on average. Besides Davis finishing second to Sanders for the rushing title, Sharpe led all tight ends with 72 catches and 1,107 receiving yards. Smith added 70 catches and a team-best 1,180 yards with a whopping 12 touchdown catches. McCaffrey had 45 catches with eight going for touchdowns.

Elway was the league's seventh-rated passer after he threw for a career-best 27 touchdowns against just 11 interceptions. He made his eighth Pro Bowl. More importantly, he was on his way to leading the Broncos to their first Super Bowl championship—even if it wasn't obvious to anyone outside the locker room at the time.

CHAPTER ELEVEN

THE REVENGE TOUR

M ike Shanahan has said it a couple hundred times over the past 25 years—the devastating 1996 playoff loss to the upstart Jacksonville Jaguars was his fault. He didn't run Terrell Davis enough. He let the Jaguars beat his team at its own game by playing a physical brand of football against his Denver Broncos defense. Goodness, did he take it out on the Jaguars in the following year's first-round playoff game.

In 1997 the two teams with the best records received first-round playoff byes. In the AFC that year, the Kansas City Chiefs and the Pittsburgh Steelers got a week's rest. The Broncos as the No. 4 seed hosted the No. 5-seeded Jaguars. This time the Broncos didn't just whip the Jaguars in a late December 1997 wild-card playoff game at Mile High. They trampled them 42–17.

The Broncos ran the ball 49 times compared to just 24 passes by John Elway. He completed 16 for 223 yards and a 43-yard touchdown pass to Rod Smith in a near-flawless passing performance. But mostly Elway's primary responsibility was to hand off and watch his running backs run. And run. And run. Davis carried 31 times for a franchise postseason record 184 yards and two touchdowns. He did all that without playing the fourth quarter as he suffered a rib injury late in the third. The running back who replaced him, Derek Loville, rushed for 103 yards and two touchdowns off just 11 carries. In all the Broncos rushed for a mindboggling 310 yards and five touchdowns. How's that for imposing your will? That wasn't even the most impressive statistic. Get this: the Broncos had 40 minutes and 59 seconds of ball possession. The Jaguars only had it for 19 minutes and one second. There was no chance for Mark Brunell, Jimmy Smith, and Natrone Means to duplicate their incredible playoff performances from a year earlier.

They never had the ball.

Adam Schefter, who was the Broncos' lead beat writer for *The Denver Post* at the time, referred to Denver's "Revenge Tour '97," in his December 28, 1997, game story of the first-round playoff rout against Jacksonville. The name stuck. There weren't any T-shirts with the motivational slogan printed on the front. The catchy slogan simply fit with the Broncos' 1997 postseason run as the Chiefs and Steelers, each of whom defeated the Broncos in the back half of the regular season, would follow the Jacksonville game.

After living nearly a full year with the catastrophic setback that ruined their otherwise exemplary 1996 season, the Broncos had exorcised their Jaguars' demons. There was never a doubt. "I don't think we were worried about bouncing back," kicker Jason Elam said in the fall of 2023. "We still had everyone in place and we knew we were incredibly talented. We really thought we were going to have another run at it. And I think it helped us when we got to the playoffs. Now we were going in as a wild-card in '97, but I think we had a chip on our shoulders. We didn't take anything for granted and we were hungry. There's no other way to say it: we were hungry. We had to go into some really difficult, hostile stadiums: at Kansas City in a division game and the Pittsburgh Steelers in the AFC Championship Game. And they were all right down to the wire. And then we were huge underdogs against the Packers, all of that. I can't say for sure how '96 impacted this, but I think it made us more hungry. Who knows? Maybe if we won in '96, we might have dropped off in '97."

Here's how the Broncos got through their three AFC playoff games to reach Super Bowl XXXII and a meeting with the heavily favored Green Bay Packers.

AFC wild-card game
December 27—Broncos 42, Jacksonville Jaguars 17 at Mile High Stadium

It was cold (19-degree windchill) and windy (30 mph with gusts to 53 mph). Perfect weather for running the ball. Alex Gibbs' offensive line took a few games to come together, as would be expected considering star left tackle Gary Zimmerman came out of retirement prior to the third game of the season. But looking back, that 38–3 rout of the San Diego Chargers in the regular-season finale was telling. Even without the injured Terrell Davis, the Denver Broncos rushed for 130 yards with their backup running backs. Elway and backup quarterback Bubby Brister combined for 35 pass attempts without getting sacked. "When you're going through it at the time, you're really good, you're winning, you've got a great coaching staff," Gary Kubiak said in the fall of 2023. "But then you take a few years away from it and you say, 'Holy (bleep), we had Zimmerman, we had Nalen, we had Schlereth, we had Sharpe.' And you start looking at the people who were playing and the team and you go, 'Hell, man, that was just amazing.' But obviously Terrell became a key piece to the team and the confidence of the team and how it was built and what we were doing and what it could do for John."

The offensive line play was absurdly good against Jacksonville. From left to right: Zimmerman, Mark Schlereth, Tom Nalen, Brian Habib, and Tony Jones were not large by NFL blocker standards, but they were quick and agile. Collectively, the offensive line cleared the way for the Broncos' offense to amass 511 total yards with a franchise playoff-record 310 on the ground.

According to the *Colorado Springs Gazette-Telegraph*, Mike Shanahan made a point of shaking every lineman's hand after the game as he informed them of that rushing total. "That's what happens when you run the ball," Zimmerman said as Shanahan joined in the laughter.

"I tell you what—and I mean this when I say it—that is the best I've ever seen an offensive line play," Elway said after the game. "They dominated the line of scrimmage from the get-go—not only the running game but the passing game. I've never seen an offensive line play better than they did today."

AFC divisional playoff game
January 4—Broncos 14, Kansas City Chiefs 10 at Arrowhead Stadium

The play of the game came on the second play of the fourth quarter. John Elway hit Ed McCaffrey on a short crossing route with the receiver doing the rest for a 43-yard catch-and-run to the Kansas City Chiefs' 1-yard line. Terrell Davis, who missed a few plays in the first half because of an aggravated rib injury suffered the week before against Jacksonville, scored from there for the game-winning points.

Davis pounded out 70 of his 101 yards in the second half. The Denver Broncos D then held up as the Chiefs self-destructed behind poor time management on their final drive. Chiefs quarterback Elvis Grbac started at his own 17-yard line with 4:04 remaining. He did a nice job getting the ball to the Denver 28 with 1:51 remaining. But the Chiefs had no timeouts, and three completed passes netted just eight yards to the Denver 20 as the clock ticked inside 20 seconds. On fourth and 2, Grbac threw a pass in the end zone that Darrien Gordon batted away.

Former Chief-turned-Bronco defensive lineman Neil Smith stood at midfield of Arrowhead Stadium, holding his Denver helmet high as Kansas City's fans booed him one more time. "When we lost to San Francisco, the Chiefs felt like they were the kings, and they were," Smith said afterward. "But they aren't anymore. I know how they're feeling right now. It just wasn't their day. I also think when you put too much emphasis on winning the AFC West and having home-field, it's easier to fall short. This is why I came to Denver because this is not our ultimate goal. When you're my age [31], nothing else matters. And if our defense can keep playing like we did today, it can happen for us."

Broncos defensive tackle Keith Traylor, who also played for the Chiefs before joining the Broncos, received a game ball from Mike Shanahan. Traylor's mother, Vernita, passed away the Friday night before the playoff game in his hometown Malvern, Arkansas. She was only 45. "I've been through a lot of adversity in life but nothing like this," Keith Traylor said to the *Colorado Springs Gazette-Telegraph*. "It's been tough, man. I loved her so much."

After the Broncos arrived in Kansas City on Saturday afternoon, the team arranged for another plane to take Traylor to see his family about 350 miles from Kansas City. He flew home, came back late Saturday night, and played one of his best games Sunday. "It really meant a lot to me that they got me a jet and flew me down there," he said. "That tells you something about the kind of people in this organization."

The Broncos had exacted revenge for their two big losses to Jacksonville in the 1996 playoffs and Kansas City in the 1997 regular season that cost them the AFC West title and home-field advantage in the postseason. Denver needed retaliation against one other team that beat them: the Pittsburgh Steelers. The loss to the Steelers in Game 14 of the regular season was still fresh. For the AFC Championship Game, the Broncos would return to Pittsburgh for the rematch. This time, the Denver defense had an answer to Pittsburgh's dual-threat quarterback Kordell Stewart.

AFC Championship Game
January 11—Broncos 24, Pittsburgh Steelers 21 at Three Rivers Stadium

The difference between the Denver Broncos and Pittsburgh Steelers was the difference between Kordell Stewart and John

Elway. A third-year pro, Stewart threw two interceptions in the end zone and also lost a fumble, while the 15-year veteran Elway was never better than when the Broncos were backed up to their 15-yard line with two minutes to go.

Desperately needing to convert a third and 6 to run out the clock, Elway received the "All Thunder" call from Mike Shanahan. The problem was tight end Shannon Sharpe didn't know the play. The play called for all receivers to run a hook pattern just past the sticks. Sharpe didn't know that. He asked Elway in the huddle what he should do. Elway told him to run out and get open. Sharpe ran a simple curl pattern. Elway delivered the ball, and after a brief bobble, Sharpe hauled it in and made 18 yards to run out the clock. Elway called it one of the biggest passes he has thrown, and Sharpe labeled it one of his biggest catches. "But we're not happy just getting back there," Elway said afterward. "We're not satisfied yet. If we win the next one, then we'll be satisfied. I think this is as good a football team all around as I've been on, and hopefully we've saved our best for last."

After living with three Super Bowl blowouts for the past eight years of his career, Elway would get a fourth chance to prove he could win the big one. "Lots of teams think it's great just to get to the Super Bowl," Elway said. "But I've had that experience, and it's not enough. We're excited, but we're not done. We're going there to win it. All I ever asked for, all

I ever wanted, was another chance. If we go in there and it doesn't work out, so be it. But this is the best team I've been around, and our work's not done. You can't win unless you go…And you can't be world champs unless you face it. We're not done…We've still got one more thing to do…One more."

It wouldn't be easy. The Green Bay Packers were the defending Super Bowl champions. Their quarterback Brett Favre had just won his third consecutive game MVP award. The NFC had won 13 Super Bowls in a row, and three of those wins came in blowout fashion against the Broncos. Elway's own mother expressed misgivings about a return trip to the Super Bowl. The Packers opened as 13-point favorites. But as Elway said, you can't win if you don't go.

CHAPTER TWELVE

THE HELICOPTER

Even against a defense that featured the incomparable Reggie White, Denver Broncos head coach Mike Shanahan, who was affectionately dubbed as The Mastermind, devised a Super Bowl XXXII game plan that would neutralize Green Bay Packers strong safety Leroy Butler.

Dominant as White still was at 36 years old, he could be cordoned off as a left defensive end. The Broncos would occasionally chip him with an extra blocker perhaps. But right tackle Tony Jones kept him sackless. The Broncos' entire offensive line kept Green Bay's defense sackless. John Elway felt pressure a time or two, sure, but by hook or crook or helicopter (sorry), he managed to slip his way free.

Shanahan, though, felt Butler was the key to the Packers' defense. Butler was a safety who was closer to playing a monster back-type role in the way Troy Polamalu would several years later for the Pittsburgh Steelers. Butler, who in 2022 was inducted into the Pro Football Hall of Fame, was sensational in the Packers' Super Bowl XXXI championship season of 1996, registering five interceptions and 149 return yards; 90 of those came on a touchdown return. He also had 6.5 sacks and 87 tackles to become arguably the league's most disruptive defensive player. In helping the Packers return to the Super Bowl in 1997, Butler made a career-high 103 tackles while having his third consecutive five-interception season. He was a first-team All-Pro for the third time. He would come from the A gap, the B gap, the C gap. He was all over the field. "Butler was the guy we game planned around," Elway said in November 2023. "He caused so much havoc inside. So we split the tight end out all the time so he couldn't do that."

The Packers opened as 13-point favorites partly because they were the defending Super Bowl champs but mostly because they were an NFC team, and the NFC had won the past 13 Super Bowls. Elway's Broncos were AFC patsies three times during the NFC's win streak, losing by an average score of 45–13. The oddsmakers' line moved down to 12 points by game time, but that didn't appear to be enough when on the game's opening series Packers running back Dorsey Levens had carries for 13 and 11 yards, and quarterback Brett Favre connected with receiver Antonio Freeman for completions of 13 and 22 yards—the last for a touchdown. Before Elway got the ball in his fourth Super Bowl appearance, he was down 7–0.

Here we go again. *Not.* "I remember sitting next to Shannon on the bench when Antonio scored on the first drive," said Broncos receiver Rod Smith. "We got together on the sideline and said, 'They got seven. Let's go get eight.' That was our mentality that day."

The Broncos answered on their first drive with a steady dose of Terrell Davis' four-yard runs before he popped a big gainer for 27. On second and 8 from the Packers' 12, Elway scrambled for 10 yards, setting up first and goal. Davis took it in a play later, and it was 7–7.

This game was also a rematch of a regular-season contest that the Packers won 41–6 at Lambeau Field on December 8, 1996, the week after the 12–1 Broncos had clinched the No. 1 AFC playoff seed and the first week in which the Broncos were permitted to rest on their laurels. Favre threw for four touchdowns, including three to Freeman, who had nine catches for 175 yards that day. "You look at Super Bowl XXXII, a big part of winning that game was us getting our ass kicked in '96 in December when we played there," recalled left guard Mark Schlereth. "They walked into that [Super Bowl XXXII] game saying, 'They can't play with us'…We walked into that game going, 'You guys got our JV team.' Terrell didn't play. Aaron Craver and Vaughn Hebron played that game. Billy Moose [Musgrave] played that game. Gary Zimmerman didn't play that game. I was a week off knee surgery. We had a bunch of other guys that didn't play. So you got our JV squad, and we were like, 'You guys are completely underestimating us.'"

The Packers got the ball for their second series of Super Bowl XXXII, but on their second play, Favre was picked off by safety Tyrone Braxton. The Broncos' second series would start at Green Bay's 45. Again, Shanahan called on a steady diet of Davis. He carried for 16 yards on the first play, then Elway hit Shannon Sharpe for nine. Davis carried four more times for short gains to end the first quarter with Denver on the Green Bay 1-yard line for third and goal.

One problem. A big problem. Davis went to the sideline between quarters saying he couldn't see. He was blinded by a migraine, an ailment he had dealt with all his life but had been under control thanks to the care of the Broncos' medical team. He had not had a migraine episode since October of 1996. But as the Broncos were near the goal line in a tie game to start the second quarter—in the Super Bowl mind you, which was played in T.D.'s hometown of San Diego—the migraine had returned with a throbbing, blinding vengeance. "It started in the first quarter," Davis recalled in November 2023. "There's a play where I get a toss to the right. Santana Dotson kind of sticks his leg out. I'm running right, trying to cut back left. I'm trying to stick him to his block, and he can't get off his block so he sticks his leg out and he trips me, and I fall, and it was a straight blow to my head. That was the beginning of it."

A day or two after the game, team doctors and head trainer Steve "Greek" Antonopulos described Davis' condition as "onset aura." He needed to go to the locker room for oxygen and drug therapy via nasal drip. The medical team was confident his migraine would clear in 15 to 30 minutes. *Fine, but what about third and goal at the 1?*

Shanahan called for Elway to play-action roll right and hit fullback Howard Griffith in the flat, but he needed Davis in the game so the Packers' defense would think he was getting the ball. Davis went out there unable to see, but his presence worked. Elway rolled right, and there was no defender around him or Griffith, who was wide open a couple yards into the right side of the end zone. Not trusting himself to make such a short pass, Elway kept it and ran it in himself.

The Broncos were up 14–7. At that point, Davis the unstoppable running back, and Davis, the decoy, would be in the locker room for the rest of the second quarter. "So I'm in the locker room for the entire second quarter after the one decoy play and halftime," Davis said nearly 26 years after the game. "What I'm hoping happens is my vision comes back. I can deal with the headaches. Believe me: I've played with headaches when I was in high school, Pop Warner without any relief. So I had experience with migraines with no relief in games. But this game I'm having some relief with pain management medication, but I can't fight through it when I can't see. Fortunately, the length of the halftime show allowed the vision to come back."

Here's to the 40th anniversary tribute to Motown for the Super Bowl XXXII halftime show. The Temptations, Smokey

Robinson, Boyz II Men, Queen Latifah, and Martha Reeves were all deserving of Super Bowl XXXII replica rings.

With Davis missing in the second quarter, the Broncos' offense predictably stalled. It would get only three more points thanks to a defensive turnover and Jason Elam's strong leg. Broncos safety Steve Atwater sacked Favre on a blitz, causing the Packers quarterback to cough up a fumble for his second turnover in as many series. The Broncos had the ball at the Packers' 33. Three plays later—again with T.D. in the locker room—the Broncos were still at the 33, but that was close enough for Elam. He nailed a 51-yard field goal for a 17–7 Broncos lead.

Favre did bounce back to direct a 17-play, 95-yard touchdown drive that ate up nearly the final 7:30 of the first half. His six-yard touchdown pass to tight end Mark Chmura made it 17–14 Broncos at halftime. Elway had only 27 yards passing on 5-of-9 completions in the first half. Davis had 64 yards rushing on nine carries in the first quarter. The Broncos needed Davis, and fortunately his vision cleared, and he was able to play the second half.

But as often happens with heroes, Davis first had to rally from a momentary lapse as a goat. The bad kind of goat—not the G.O.A.T. he would later be called in Broncos' annals. On the first play of the second half, Davis fumbled the ball away. Green Bay had the ball at the Broncos' 26. But just as it appeared the Packers had flipped momentum, they committed back-to-back false start penalties and had to settle for a short Ryan Longwell field goal and a 17–17 tie.

The teams then exchanged punts. Then The Helicopter was upon us.

With 7:46 left in the third quarter, Elway finally started to heat up to give Davis some help. Starting at his own 8-yard line, Elway sandwiched completions of eight yards to Sharpe and 36 yards to Ed McCaffrey between Davis runs of four, four, and seven yards. The Broncos had moved from their own 8 to the Packers' 33. Then it was Davis again for eight yards, Elway to McCaffrey again for nine more. First down at the Packers' 16. Two more Davis runs made it third and 6 at the Green Bay 12.

In Elway's first 14 seasons, he had The Drive, but he didn't have a Super Bowl title. In this game he would have his iconic play, The Helicopter, and he would have his championship.

"Here's the funny thing about the Helicopter. I say this all the time: Mike had put this play in for the red zone," Elway said at breakfast in November 2023. "And I didn't really like it in practice. And I told Mike, 'I don't like this play.' I didn't like it against the defense he had it set up against. It was real tight, and I didn't feel good about it. He said, 'Against this formation and this situation, it's 100 percent they will be in this defense. One hundred percent.' Sure enough, it's third and 6, and here comes the play."

Shanahan knew his quarterback wasn't happy with the play call he sent in. "When I gave him the play, I can tell he's looking at me like he's giving me the finger," Shanahan said at his steakhouse table 26 years later. "He wanted to, but then he thought twice because of all the people watching. But he wanted to, I promise you."

Elway laughed when told what Shanahan said about the bird. Instead, Elway gave Shanahan a you-got-to-be-kidding-me look. "And they're not in that defense," Elway said. "So I say, 'All right, I'm going to let the rush come and try to get outside and try to get somebody open.' Somebody went high, and I went inside-out."

Now nearly 26 years later, Shanahan said he did have a built-in provision in case the Packers didn't play the defense he anticipated. But he had his reasons for not telling Elway. "What I didn't tell John—what I didn't tell him until 10 years later—you couldn't tell John everything about a play because he didn't have the patience," Shanahan said. "He was, 'Just tell me what to do.' The night before, I said, 'If they're playing off and we're in shotgun, take a quick five-step drop, and you run the quarterback draw.' What I told our linemen was: I didn't want anybody going downfield."

Defensive players key off the offensive linemen, not the ball. If the offensive line blocks forward, it's a run. If the blockers back off and set up on their haunches, it's a pass. That way, defenders don't get fooled by ball fakes or misdirections. The offensive line is the tell. "I didn't want John to know that nobody was blocking the linebacker," Shanahan said, "because John didn't like the play to start with. I did not want to throw the ball in that situation. I wanted to get it inside the 4-yard line. It set up perfect. I'm hoping he goes five steps. I was afraid he was going to go three and take off right away. But he gets the ball and he takes a quick five-step drop. I'm looking at the center and the guard, and the left guard, Schlereth, is uncovered. He and the center do a great job setting. And when John took a five-step drop, those linebackers all took off into the end zone. What they were looking for is one of the lineman going downfield on the quarterback draw. When I saw that, I know John's going to make it. And that's how the whirlybird came around. It winds up being one of the plays he's noted for."

McCaffrey and Smith were running routes on the play when Elway took off. "When I did turn around and saw him taking off, you can't block somebody fast enough," McCaffrey said. "I do remember the feeling of, *Oh my gosh, I better block somebody. He's running.*"

Jones, the Broncos right tackle, did a nice job guiding White, the superstar defensive end to the outside. White was one of only three pass rushers the Packers sent on the play. The rest dropped into coverage. Elway stepped up into the pocket and cut right. He got inside the 10 and started his leap forward at about the seven, one yard shy of the first down. He knew he was going to hit. "Oh yeah, I said, 'This is the only way I've got a chance,'" Elway said, "because the one guy went low. So the only way I could get the first down was to get that six-inch vertical on them and go right over the top."

It was Packers linebacker Brian Williams who went low on Elway, but Williams came up empty. Elway had leapt just high enough to miss the linebacker. Butler came in from the left side and nailed Elway on his right hip just as backup safety Mike Prior was coming in from Elway's left. Prior clipped Elway's lowered left shoulder, spinning the quarterback around. Elway landed at the four.

First and goal. The simultaneous hits actually seemed to spin Elway higher into the air. Way higher than six inches. "They did," he said. "It was funny because I was discombobulated and wasn't sure where I ended up. Then I stood up to see where I was. Then I looked to our sideline, and our sideline was going nuts. I mean, I can still feel how I felt—the adrenaline rush like I never had before."

McCaffrey said The Helicopter brought an extra degree of energy to the game and the team. "Absolutely, yeah, there was a feeling of excitement," he said. "You always have to turn the page and focus on the next play. But for a few seconds in the huddle after that play, there was an adrenaline rush for everybody. Not just in the huddle, but I'm sure on the sidelines and fans. You know those moments when you feel like it's about to happen? That's what it felt like."

Smith had a unique view. "I had a front-row seat watching it," he said. "It was a pass play. So I'm running my route into the end zone, running across to my left. There's a picture of me in the background when he's spinning, and I'm looking at him propelling in the air and I'm really looking for the ball. When he got hit from this side, and somebody else hit him from the other side, I thought that ball might come out. So I'm standing there, and you'll see me leaning forward, and then as soon as he hit the ground, I saw he had the ball. We both looked to the side to see he had the first down by about a yard, yard and a half. And then that energy in that huddle, it was crazy. It became a signature moment for him and it was also a signature moment for the Broncos because here's this guy, I think he's 37 years old, but he could still move. The rest of us had the scramble drill and once you see him tucking, you go get a guy to keep him off him. I saw him take every hit that he took and I'm just glad he held on to the ball. I wouldn't say that's when it turned for us because I felt like we were in control the whole game."

Prior to Elway's signature play, Elam was bracing for either a field goal or extra-point try. "I was really close to it because I was getting ready," Elam said. "I remember him getting up and looking to us and raising his fist up, and it was like, 'Okay, if Green Bay is going to win, they're going to have to bleed for it because we were all in.' At that point— everybody—we were already committed, but it was just this feeling that we are going down swinging."

Davis took it in two plays later, and the Broncos were up 24–17.

On third and 6 with 36 seconds left in the game and the Broncos protecting a 31–24 lead, Atwater delivered a blast would have drawn a 15-yard flag today, and his own team-mate, Randy Hilliard, received the brunt of the blow. "You look at that Steve Atwater hit," Elam said. "He took himself out, one of the other DBs out, and [Robert Brooks] out. We were going to lay it all on the field that game. That was just the leadership of John [Elway] modeling that for us in giving up his body, and we're going to follow suit."

A groggy Atwater had to come out and watch from the sideline as Favre threw a final fourth-down pass behind Chmura. Broncos linebacker John Mobley was able to knock it down. Ballgame. Broncos won 31–24.

Davis was the Super Bowl XXXII MVP after rushing for 157 yards—93 in the second half after he came back from his blinding migraine—and three touchdowns. Elway was just 12-of-22 for 123 yards with no passing touchdowns and an interception in the game. He had far better passing stats in his first Super Bowl game against the New York Giants. But unlike Super Bowl XXI against the Giants, Elway won so much more in XXXII. "This is what I've played for all these years," Elway said after the game. "There have been a lot of questions over me with the three Super Bowl losses, being in the league 15 years and getting labeled as a guy who has never been on a winning Super Bowl team, the NFC-AFC thing for the last 13 years, even all the quarterbacks from the class of '83 who never won a championship—all those questions. But those questions are gone now. All of them."

Elway had the stats, the records, the Pro Bowls, The Drive, the AFC championships, and then in his 15th season, The Helicopter and his Super Bowl ring. He had done it all. "It's the unselfishness," Schlereth said. "You look at John, and Mike said, 'Hey, John, you're not going to be the MVP of Super Bowl XXXII. But if you want to win it, this is what we need to do.' One thing that was intriguing with John about that part of his career was zero ego. *What do we have to do to win?* Our Friday practice going into our first Super Bowl was the sharpest, quickest practice we had since we had been here under Mike Shanahan. Not a ball hit the ground. There was not repeated play. It was like clockwork. The game plan was about dominating the line of scrimmage, about running the football, about formationally putting them in a place where we could exploit them. It wasn't about John throwing the football. We knew the history of John. We knew the history of the Broncos."

But Elway wasn't done. After starving for a Super Bowl title through the first 14 seasons of his career, Elway would keep eating once he was fed. "In '97 we won it for John," Denver defensive tackle Maa Tanuvasa said at the 25-year reunion of the 1998 Super Bowl in September 2023. "And in '98 we won it for us."

Why win it for Elway in 1997? "Because growing up I saw him going to Super Bowls and get disappointed," Tanuvasa said. "But to be led by a leader like that through my years that I was here in Denver, [I] just knew that he was hungry for one. So that was for John. Just like Pat Bowlen said: that was for John."

Bubby Brister, Elway's backup quarterback, also attended the 25-year reunion of the 1997 Super Bowl team. Unprompted, Brister went right to what he remembered most about the Broncos' Super Bowl XXXII win. "When John helicoptered there at the end when we were playing the Packers, it was probably the highlight of the whole deal," Brister said, "because there was this energy all through the sidelines and all of the fans. We felt we could win at that point."

CHAPTER THIRTEEN

THIS ONE'S FOR JOHN

P at Bowlen was able to summon his usual dose of poise and calm to mask his discomfort.

For the first time in his life, Bowlen was on a national stage. He held a commanding presence while speaking with authority at local press conferences in those rare times he hired or fired a coach or introduced new uniforms. This time there were 69,000 people gathered at San Diego's Qualcomm Stadium on January 25, 1998 and estimates of another 133 million watching at home or in sports bars. After 14 years as the Denver Broncos owner, after spending every possible revenue dollar to give his team every resource in the pursuit of ultimate victory, after demonstrating great loyalty to two head coaches and one quarterback, Bowlen was finally getting his due. The Broncos had just won their first ever Super Bowl title.

They earned it by pulling off a monumental upset against the 12-point favorite Green Bay Packers to snap the NFC's 13-year Super Bowl win streak. It was an enthralling game in part because it was error-filled. There were five turnovers, including three by the Packers. After John Elway's Helicopter set up the Broncos' go-ahead touchdown for a 24–17 lead late in the third quarter, there were turnovers on back-to-back plays. Star Packers receiver Antonio Freeman fumbled away the ensuing kickoff return, giving Denver the ball at the Packers' 22 and a chance to put the game away; Elway promptly got picked off by Eugene Robinson at the 2-yard line on the very next play.

From there Brett Favre got in a Favre groove, going 4-for-4 in a four-play, 85-yard drive—a 25-yard pass interference penalty against Darrien Gordon helped—to tie it 24–24 less than two minutes into the fourth quarter. The Packers' answer to Terrell Davis was Freeman, who had nine catches for 126 yards and two touchdowns. But by game's end, the Packers had no answer for T.D.

With 5:25 remaining in regulation, the Broncos' Tom Rouen lofted a punt to the 11-yard line. The Packers couldn't move the ball because of two penalties against left tackle Ross Verba—a holding and false start call—and a poor third-and-11 throw by Favre to an open Freeman. A short punt by Craig Hentrich gave Denver the ball at the Green Bay 49 with 3:27 remaining. Tie game, 24–24. As Broncos' radio play-by-play man Dave Logan would say, "Here we go."

The Packers' defensive front, anchored by the massive Gilbert Brown, was spent. The Broncos wore them down with nearly five more minutes in time of possession. A big factor in the game was that the Packers lost starting right defensive end Gabe Wilkins to a knee injury on the Broncos' first series. The Broncos frequently attacked his replacement, Darius Holland. On the first play from near midfield, a short Davis run drew a 15-yard facemask penalty against Holland. Elway then threw a swing pass to fullback Howard Griffith for 23 yards, and at the two-minute warning, the Broncos had first and goal at the 8.

Davis ran for seven yards, but tight end Shannon Sharpe was called for holding. First and goal at the 18. No problem. Davis ran through a gaping hole inside left end for 17 yards. Second and goal at the 1. Packers coach Mike Holmgren admitted later he thought it was first and goal after the Davis' 17-yard run. So he decided to purposely let Davis score from the 1-yard line, knowing the Broncos would go ahead 31–24 but also giving Favre one minute, 47 seconds to drive for the tying score and play for overtime. Favre did drive the Packers to the Broncos' 31, but the series ended there. Elway kneeled out the final second from the Victory Formation.

"My favorite moment in football," Broncos receiver Ed McCaffrey said years later when asked about the highlight of his 13-year career.

Then Greg Gumbel, the emcee of the Lombardi Trophy presentation, introduced Bowlen to receive the coveted Lombardi hardware. "There's one thing I want to say here tonight," Bowlen said in a composed manner despite his reluctance. "It's only four words."

He then picked up the Lombardi Trophy that was resting on a platform. Bowlen raised the invaluable relic high above his head with his right hand and exalted in perfect rhythm: "This…one's…for…John!"

The ensuing years would germinate that brief but profound acceptance speech into iconic proportions. Given his rightful place beneath the brightest of spotlights, Bowlen couldn't wait to step away. All he wanted to do was to redirect all attention to his quarterback and all-time favorite player, Elway.

Davis was the game's Most Valuable Player. The offensive line—deemed too small by NFL analysts to take on Reggie White, Brown, and the massive Green Bay defensive front—had opened up gaping holes in the run game and kept Elway spotless in the passing game. The Greg Robinson-coached defense was a heavy blitzing machine that rattled Favre into a subpar performance. Mike Shanahan was The Mastermind behind rebuilding the Broncos from the 7–9 also-ran operation he inherited to their first Super Bowl championship in three years.

Elway only threw for 123 yards with no touchdowns. Yet, Bowlen's affinity for his quarterback would not be suppressed. This. One's. For. John! "Surprised? Yeah, I had no idea that was coming," Elway said of Bowlen's speech. "I was a little

Standing next to his father, Jack, Stanford University quarterback John Elway announces on April 26, 1983 that he would rather play baseball for the New York Yankees than sign with the Baltimore Colts.

Pittsburgh Steelers Jack Lambert (58) and Loren Toews (51) tackle quarterback John Elway during his NFL debut. The rookie completed just 1-of-8 passes for 14 yards while getting sacked four times.

Denver Broncos running back Steve Sewell sets up a first and goal during the Broncos' 23–20 overtime victory against the Cleveland Browns in the 1986 AFC Championship Game.

To cap "The Drive," Denver Broncos wide receiver Mark Jackson celebrates after his five-yard touchdown sends the AFC Championship Game into overtime on January 11, 1987.

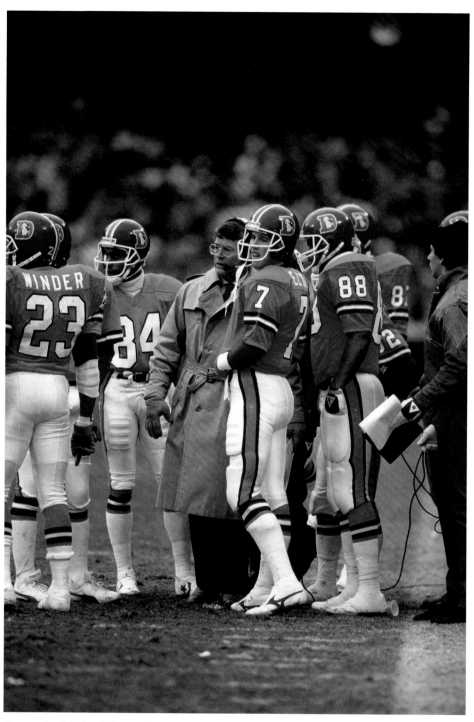

Quarterback John Elway, who often didn't see eye to eye with his head coach, talks with Dan Reeves during the Broncos' 23–20 overtime victory against the Cleveland Browns.

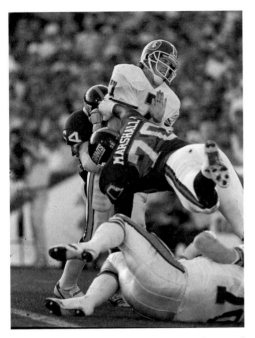

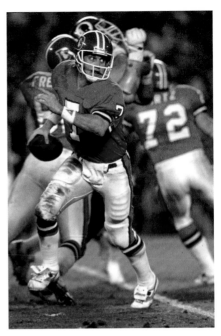

New York Giants defensive linemen Leonard Marshall (70) and Jim Burt (64) pummel quarterback John Elway during the second quarter of the Denver Broncos' 39–20 loss in Super Bowl XXI.

Quarterback John Elway tries to avoid pressure during the Denver Broncos' second consecutive Super Bowl loss. The Washington Redskins ended up winning this one 42–10.

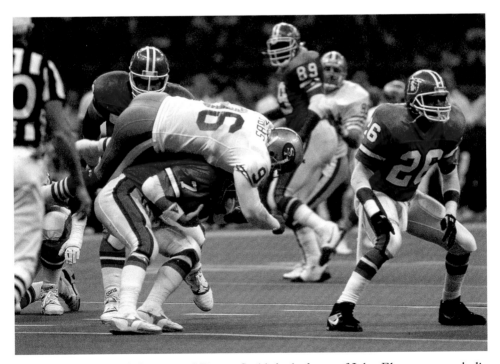

San Francisco 49ers defensive end Danny Stubbs' takedown of John Elway was symbolic of the 55–10 beatdown in Super Bowl XXIV.

Mike Shanahan, who had a much better relationship with John Elway than Dan Reeves did, talks to his quarterback during his first season as Denver Broncos head coach in 1995.

The addition of running back Terrell Davis, a future Pro Football Hall of Famer, made life much easier for John Elway.

From left to right, offensive coordinator Gary Kubiak, head coach Mike Shanahan, and quarterback John Elway observe the action during the Broncos' 34–0 defeat of the Carolina Panthers in 1997.

As part of "The Helicopter"—the signature play of Super Bowl XXXII—John Elway takes on three Green Bay Packers defenders while converting a third down late in the third quarter.

After losing his first three Super Bowls, John Elway celebrates the Denver Broncos' 31–24 victory in Super Bowl XXXII.

In the game-changing play of Super Bowl XXXIII, Denver Broncos wide receiver Rod Smith beats embattled Atlanta Falcons safety Eugene Robinson for an 80-yard touchdown in the second quarter.

Denver Broncos head coach Mike Shanahan got the best of his former boss, Atlanta Falcons head coach Dan Reeves, after the Broncos won Super Bowl XXXIII 34–19.

John Elway, who passed for 336 yards in the victory, celebrates his second straight Super Bowl title.

From left to right, Denver Broncos owner Pat Bowlen, Peyton Manning, and general manager John Elway pose during a 2012 press conference announcing the signing of the former Indianapolis Colts quarterback.

Denver Broncos quarterback Peyton Manning and general manager John Elway embrace after defeating the New England Patriots 20–18 in the AFC Championship Game to earn a spot in Super Bowl 50.

embarrassed because everybody had put in so much work, and it was nice to get over the hump. But it was also nice for Pat to say that."

That moment—immediately passing all glory to Elway—encapsulated Pat Bowlen's Hall of Fame legacy as the Broncos owner. "That's Mr. B," said Steve Atwater, an eight-time Pro Bowl safety in his 10 seasons with the Broncos who in 2020 was elected into the Pro Football Hall of Fame. "He never wanted the focus to be on himself. He always wanted his team and his coaches and his trainers—everybody else to get all the credit. He never wanted credit. A lot of us, we can learn from that. He was a very effective leader. We all loved him."

* * *

Pat Bowlen was also a shrewd businessman. When you buy a team for $71 million in 1984 and then the franchise passes on to your beneficiaries for $4.65 *billion* in 2022, you know how to run a business. Immediately after winning Super Bowl XXXII, Bowlen sought to capitalize on the local citizens' emotion to get a taxpayer-funded new stadium on the ballot first and then approved by voters second. "We showed we deserve it," Bowlen told the *Rocky Mountain News* at the team's Super Bowl victory parade. "I hope to get it [on the ballot] as soon as possible because I think we deserve it. I never doubted the people of Colorado and fans will vote for this stadium. We need it to be competitive."

Mile High Stadium was one of the loudest outdoor venues in all of sports. There's no doubt it helped provide the Denver Broncos—along with 5,280 feet of rarefied air—a tremendous home-field advantage. But new stadiums were popping up around the country, most notably down the street where Coors Field gave the Colorado Rockies' baseball team nearly 100 percent of the revenues on tickets, parking, and concessions. The Broncos had to share too big a percentage with the city and county of Denver on its tickets, concessions, and parking revenues.

Plus, Bowlen needed the real money maker that are luxury suites. According to a 1994 Longo Report, which was a 14-month engineering study of Mile High Stadium, it was going to cost $264 million (in 1994 dollars) for upkeep of Mile High Stadium through the end of the Broncos' lease in 2018. That report sparked negotiations for a new stadium, which resulted in a vote on Tuesday, November 3, 1998. The vote asked taxpayers if they would extend the 0.1 percent sales tax that built Coors Field—and was already paid off—to fund a new stadium for the Broncos. Bowlen started campaigning for a new stadium in 1994, repeatedly stating the only way the Broncos could remain competitive was by finding a way to stay on the same financial playing field as other teams. A month before the election, Bowlen had provided $650,000 of the $1.4 million that Citizens for a New Stadium (CFANS) was spending.

Citizens Opposed to the Stadium Tax collected a total of $23,800. Money rules in every arena. In the end Bowlen said the Broncos spent about $5 million over four years to win the new stadium's election. It passed with 57 percent of the vote. The 0.1 percent Coors Field sales tax was extended to 2012 to build a football stadium. "You bet it was worth it!" Bowlen said at a rally after the election. Bowlen agreed with estimates his team was worth $100 million more overnight thanks to the election. "If I'm going to spend $130 million, I sure hope it's going to raise [the value of the team] by $100 million," he said.

The stadium campaign is when Bowlen was at his best. "He was very, very shy," Mike Shanahan told 9NEWS after Bowlen passed away in June 2019 following a long battle with Alzheimer's. "I would tell people: 'Really, he's a pretty good guy, he's just really shy.' He got embarrassed when he didn't know people's names. I said, 'Pat, people don't care if you don't know their name as long as you're nice to them.' But I thought when we started going for the stadium, he really started coming out of his shell. He'd meet people. He had a cause to talk to people. I thought he did one heck of a job."

It didn't hurt that his defending Super Bowl championship team was 8–0 to begin the 1998 season at the time of the early November vote. A voting majority agreed to fund 75 percent of what became a $400 million new stadium. Initially named Invesco Field at Mile High when it opened on September 10, 2001—the night before the 9/11 terrorist attacks on our country—the 76,125-seat Broncos' stadium was renamed Sports Authority Field at Mile High in 2011.

It is now called Empower Field at Mile High. The Broncos' sellout streak was approaching 450 consecutive home games, including playoffs, after the 2023 season. The NFL's longest active streak, it dates back 54 seasons to 1970.

For his incredible success with not only the Broncos, but also as a lead partner in helping grow the NFL into the gargantuan universe that dwarfs all other sports, Bowlen was inducted into the Pro Football Hall of Fame. Elected while still alive but in declining health after years of battling Alzheimer's, Bowlen passed away from the disease in June 2019, two months before his induction. Bowlen more than earned his football immortality. From the time he bought the team in March 1984 until he relinquished his duties with the announcement in July 2014 he was battling Alzheimer's disease, the Broncos in that 30-season period astonishingly had more Super Bowl appearances (six) than losing seasons (five). He had reached three Super Bowls with Dan Reeves, Bowlen's head coach for nine seasons, two with Mike Shanahan, his head coach for 14 seasons, and one with John Fox.

Bowlen's Broncos would add a seventh Super Bowl appearance and a third Lombardi Trophy in 2015 under head coach Gary Kubiak and quarterback Peyton Manning. Bowlen may not have been in charge when the Broncos won Super Bowl 50 to cap the 2015 season, but he deserves credit for leaving the Denver franchise in the trusted hands of longtime team executive Joe Ellis and John Elway, who had become the team's general manager and built the roster. Through his Broncos' reign alone, Bowlen was a Hall of Famer. He was after all the first single owner in NFL history to record 300 wins in 30 seasons.

Ah, but there was so much more. Bowlen's influence on growing the National Football League into the $15 billion-a-year entertainment enterprise it is today was equally impressive. He chaired the NFL's television committee from the late 1980s through the mid-1990s, a time when the media dollars grew exponentially. Bowlen was the reasoned voice representing ownership when it came to resolving often contentious collective bargaining negotiations (with the players union) into a peaceful resolution. He was at the forefront of the league's new stadium movement by stomping for local funding and the construction of what is now Empower Field at Mile High, which was among the league's first venues in the new wave in the 2000s decade. And Bowlen was the first to raise his hand when the NFL wanted to play international preseason games in the 1980s and 1990s. "There were four areas where the league was really transformed in the late '80s, early '90s," said Paul Tagliabue, who started his long run as NFL commissioner in 1989. "Pat was the only owner who was heavily involved in all four areas."

Deserving as he was, Bowlen would have said there was a problem with his election into the Hall of Fame: it's an individual honor. It may be the most glorious individual award one can ever receive, but Bowlen would not have liked getting singled out. "I know what he would say," said Ellis, Bowlen's right-hand man for more than 20 years who later became the team's owner delegee for 10 seasons. "He would say, 'Why isn't [Randy] Gradishar in? And why is [Karl] Mecklenburg not in? And why is [Steve] Atwater not in? And why isn't Tom Nalen in? And why isn't Rod Smith in? And we need more Broncos players in there because the players are the thing.' That's how he felt about it. He loved the players, and they loved him back. I know he had tremendous respect for all the players. He knew how hard their jobs were and how grueling the game was and the pressures they were under. And I think they understood that he understood that."

Since that statement Atwater and Gradishar did go into the Hall of Fame, and one of Mr. B's all-time favorite players, cornerback Champ Bailey, joined him in the Hall of Fame class of 2019. Bailey remembers how he didn't want to be traded after his fifth season with the Washington Redskins. Ten years after he was traded to Denver, he was so happy the trade happened. "After a year or two, I knew the difference was Pat Bowlen," Bailey said. "A guy who's running the team the way he runs it, you're going to have success. And I knew I had a better chance at having success in Denver than I did in Washington. And that was the best thing that happened to my career."

* * *

Patrick Dennis Bowlen was born February 18, 1944 in Prairie du Chien, Wisconsin, where he grew up and played hockey, football (as a starting receiver), and ran the 440 meters in track for Campion Jesuit Catholic High School. It was a boarding school that no longer exists.

"If we were eating at home, we would have a roast chicken," said Brittany Bowlen, one of Pat Bowlen's daughters with his wife, Annabel. "He loved roast chicken, but he hated potatoes. He used to say he ate too many of them in boarding school."

Bowlen then attended the University of Oklahoma, where he earned his business degree in 1965 and law degree in 1968. At that point he moved to Edmonton, Alberta, where he became a lawyer for his father Paul's oil company. Through his father's wildcatting success and his own resourcefulness, Pat Bowlen began building wealth through real estate, oil, and gas.

Bowlen started looking to buy a professional sports franchise and was introduced through mutual friends to then-Denver Broncos owner Edgar Kaiser Jr. In 1984 Bowlen and two of his siblings bought 60.8 percent of the Broncos for $51 million. A year after their initial purchase from Kaiser, the Bowlens bought the remaining 39.2 percent minority interest for $20 million. Bowlen eventually bought out his siblings' majority interest. That $71 million total investment grew 65 times as his estate sold the team to the Walton-Penner ownership for a staggering and then record-setting $4.65 billion via auction in August of 2022.

To put it simply, Pat Bowlen became the best owner in Denver sports history and he's among the best in any of America's four major sports. "At the end of the day, it starts at the top," said Bill Romanowski, the Broncos middle line-backer during the team's back-to-back Super Bowl titles in 1997–98. "You don't win Super Bowls with a bad owner, with an owner who doesn't care, with an owner who is just in this to make money. He gave us everything we needed to compete at the highest level. That's what it was about for him. He wanted to take care of the players so they could go out there and win games and win Super Bowls."

Bowlen didn't use the Broncos to build his own personal fortune. Yes, he wore nice clothes, drove sporty cars, and drank some of the best wine. But those expenses came after he reinvested into the franchise so that it was always within 3 to 5 percent of the payroll cap. (The 3 to 5 percent was held back in reserve to replace players that fell on injured reserve.) He wound up contributing nearly $150 million for the team's stadium construction plus another $30 million in improvements. He moved the team's headquarters in 1990 to Dove Valley and made $38 million in enhancements, including the Pat Bowlen Fieldhouse at the Broncos' training center headquarters. And the Denver Broncos Charities had donated more than $25 million to various groups from 1993 to 2019.

But Bowlen always considered his ultimate civic duty was bringing a Super Bowl contender to Denver. "This is their team," Bowlen said during a 2013 interview as he looked out from his office to his loyal training camp gathering outside. "It's not my team. I think if you manage your club well, the fans appreciate that."

His players did, too. "Man, everybody talks about their owner," said Shannon Sharpe, the Broncos' Hall of Fame tight end. "But Mr. B for me, it's hard pressed for me to believe there are better owners than Mr. Bowlen. Even before I became 'Shannon Sharpe,' he still took the time to ask me how I was doing, what was going on. Mr. B, the TV contracts, what we have with the players' association, he has been big. And sometimes because he was a quiet owner, he didn't want the spotlight, he didn't hold press conferences to tell you who was going to play. He hired the best coaches and was perfectly content to have the coach [maintain control]. He would say, 'I got the easy job. I just cut the check. They have the hard job, they're the ones that are practicing, they're the ones who are putting in the hard work.' I always admired him for that."

Even had Bowlen not received the Hall of Fame nod, his legacy would have carried on with the National Football League. Bowlen's efforts would have been there every time a viewer tuned into NBC's *Sunday Night Football*. That began with the Pro Football Hall of Fame Game in August 2006 and has been America's most watched television program since 2011. "He was the single major force in getting *Sunday Night Football*," said Dick Ebersol, the former chairman of NBC Sports. "I believe during his years as chairman of the TV committee, Pat Bowlen had more to do with how we watch football in America right now than anybody else in the league. His tough and direct manner made him someone who you just instantly had to respect. You can say he was the father of *Sunday Night Football*. It never would have happened without him."

NFL TV contracts went from $473 million a year in 1989 to $900 million in 1990. Then in 1993 with Bowlen anchoring league negotiations, FOX became a partner, and the NFL went from a large planet in American sports solar system to its own galaxy. And as the league soared, Bowlen's Broncos rode shotgun.

What was his most incredible accomplishment—six Super Bowl appearances through his 30 years as active ownership? Or just five losing seasons during that time? "That's the art of the deal right there," said Dallas Cowboys owner Jerry Jones who was inducted into the Hall of Fame as a contributor in 2017. "How do you position your team to be in it year in and year out yet at the same time in our system not go completely to the bottom? He has shown us how to do that."

Although he was born in Wisconsin and attended college at the University of Oklahoma, Bowlen had roots in Canada, and it took a while for the Denver region to warm up to the outsider. Shy by nature, Bowlen was initially perceived as aloof by the Denver region, and his image wasn't helped when he was seen wearing a fur coat on the sidelines early in his ownership tenure.

But Bowlen put away the fur coat after "The Drive" game in Cleveland in January 1987 and in time became one of the NFL's most respected and beloved owners. And productive. "Pat really made a big difference," said Dan Reeves, the Broncos coach from 1981 to 1992. "Not that Edgar Kaiser wouldn't give you whatever you needed, but Pat was more hands on. Edgar would stay away. Pat built us a new indoor facility. Before when the weather was bad, we really didn't have a place to practice. That helped us because Seattle was in our division at that time, and they had an indoor stadium. It helped us practice against them by creating noise." It's fitting then that when the Broncos built a new indoor practice field at their training center in 2015, it was named the Pat Bowlen Fieldhouse.

Each day when he showed up at Broncos headquarters, Bowlen's first stop was in the trainer's room where he would chat with head trainer Steve "Greek" Antonopulos, who worked 45 years with the team before retiring in 2021. "The most important thing to him was to know how his players were," Antonopulos said. "He cared about his players more than anyone I had ever been around. The sense of compassion he had—yeah, sure, he was the owner and he had a stake in it, but he really cared about the personal lives, cared about their injuries. He wanted to know what was going on with them. It was just amazing over the years how he developed that compassion. It was there till the last time he was around the facility. It was a major deal to him."

His management style was to show up at the office every day and make sure every decision came through his desk. Yet he balanced this active role with not interfering with people from doing their job particularly on the football side of team operations. "You knew who you were working for," Reeves said. "But all he wanted to do was reinforce to you that he would do whatever you needed."

In 1999 after John Elway retired as a player, Bowlen reportedly offered his favorite quarterback an option to buy 10 percent of the principal stock in the team. That deal hit a serious snag. A condition of Kaiser's sale to Bowlen, which would later be disputed for nearly a decade in the court system, was that Kaiser would have right of first refusal if Bowlen ever tried to sell off a portion of that majority interest. When Bowlen tried to make Elway a partner, Kaiser sued, claiming he was not offered right of first refusal. The courts ruled in Kaiser's favor in 2004, but Bowlen appealed and won in October 2008. Kaiser died in January 2012. Elway never did get the chance to buy the 10 percent, but in one of Bowlen's final decisions as owner, he hired Elway in January 2011 to take control of the Broncos' football operations department. Simultaneously, Bowlen took a step back from day-to-day operations and handed final-say authority of his club to Joe Ellis, who was promoted from chief operating officer to president.

When Bowlen formally relinquished control of the team in July 2014, Ellis was promoted again—this time to chief executive officer.

The Broncos and the Bowlen family formally announced Pat Bowlen had been declared incapacitated from Alzheimer's at a press conference prior to the start of team's 2014 training camp. Elway, the general manager, became emotional. "Having worked for him for 40 years," Elway said as his voice choked, his eyes welled, and then pausing for several seconds to try and gather himself from crying, "it's going to be very hard to not see him walk through those front doors every day."

Elway blew out a breath. He continued to speak unscripted from the heart. "He has given me so much," Elway said, his speech still halting from emotion. "As a player to be able to play for him—as I said when I retired, as a player all you want is an opportunity to be the best and be able to compete for world championships. And as a player, that's what Pat Bowlen's given us."

When the Broncos won Super Bowl 50 to cap the 2015 season, Elway in his blue suit and orange tie accepted the Lombardi Trophy as the team's general manager who built the championship roster. "This One's for Pat!" Elway shouted as he held up the hardware.

CHAPTER FOURTEEN

ONE MORE TIME

It was a confusing time. In the days after the Denver Broncos won Super Bowl XXXII, much was written and said about the possibility John Elway would retire and go out on top after finally winning his world championship. But as he looked back over breakfast 25 years later at the Perfect Landing restaurant that overlooks the private jets at Centennial Airport, Elway said he was never close to calling it a playing career after the 1997 season. "I didn't think a lot about it," Elway said.

He had always used his dad as a gauge. Jack Elway was a longtime college football coach before he became a Broncos scout for several years. Dad knew who could play and who couldn't. He was also a no-B.S., straight shooter who never sugarcoated things to his son. "I said, 'Dad, you're going to be the one who has to tell me whether I can still play or not because I'm always going to think I can,'" Elway said. "I talked to him after the Green Bay game. First, we had a real good team coming back. I was never really close to stepping away."

Elway's agent Marvin Demoff told the press on February 5, 1998—nine days after Elway and the Broncos were relieved of their burden of having never won the Big One—that

Elway would inform owner Pat Bowlen and head coach Mike Shanahan that he was coming back. By coming back to play at least one more season, Demoff said, Elway would help Bowlen get his new stadium and give Shanahan a year to find a new quarterback successor. It would also allow Elway to take a farewell tour through the NFL for one more season. Demoff's comments came a week from the start of 1998 free agency.

However, Elway said the next day he wanted more time to think it through. He sat on it for nearly four months before he first told Broncos radio color analyst Scott Hastings during the John Elway Golf Classic on May 30 that he was returning for his 16th season in 1998. He didn't officially announce he was coming back for one more season until a June 1 press conference—four months and a week after winning Super Bowl XXXII. "This is the greatest news since they found migraine medicine that works," Broncos running back Terrell Davis told *The Denver Post*. "This puts us back there with the top teams in the league. The quarterback position to me is the most important position, and to have John back? C'mon, man, I was geeked all day. I was driving around in my car all day like we won the Super Bowl. I kept saying, 'John's coming back! John's coming back!'"

Elway did make it fairly clear at his June 1 press conference that the 1998 season would be it. He said: "99.9 percent sure."

In some ways 1998 would be Elway's easiest season; in some ways it would be difficult.

Because the 1998 Broncos were undisputedly the greatest team in team history, it made it easy. They scored a league-most 501 points or 31.3 points a game. And that's with backup quarterback Bubby Brister playing the bulk of five games. The Denver D ranked No. 8 in the league by allowing 19.3 points a game, but that was misleading because a significant portion was allowed during garbage time. "I mean, it was fun," said kicker Jason Elam. "What I remember is we would be up 21–0 toward the end of the first quarter and 31–3 at halftime and just pulling back a little bit. We were dominant. It was really a fun time."

After carrying the Broncos with his big-play, impact passing and clutch fourth-quarter drives for the first dozen or so years of his career, Elway had mostly settled into a game manager role in his final years under Shanahan. Elway was efficient, but it was Davis who carried the offense. T.D. would finish with 2,008 rushing yards, which may never be topped as the greatest rushing season in Broncos history even with the schedules now expanded to 17 games. "One thing John told me once just in passing and it always kind of stuck with me is: 'Hey, your job is first and second down,'" said Broncos left guard Mark Schlereth. "'Take that off my plate. My job is to convert on third down. That's what I get paid to do.' So there's this unselfishness where I don't have to be a superstar three downs in a row. I'm fine if at the end of the day we run it for 250 yards and I only have to throw it 18 times. Great. I don't get hit, I can sleep at night, and we can celebrate a win.'" Less was more.

The hard part was that Elway was banged up throughout the 1998 season, missing four complete games and parts of two others with a strained hamstring and battered ribs. He wound up with some of the lowest passing stats in his career with 2,806 yards. But his 22 touchdown passes were among his single-season best, and his 93.0 passer rating was the best in his career.

"When John and I talked football, he had an amazing perspective on things," said Gary Kubiak, the Broncos offensive coordinator in their 1997–98 Super Bowl seasons. "He always said, 'I've got four downs to make 10 yards. I'm going to make big plays at some point.' He was extremely unselfish. He'd throw the ball way. 'Keep us at third and 10, I'll find a way to keep us on the field.' He used to always say, 'Third downs are money downs. That's what they pay me for.'"

As his career was winding down, Elway was occasionally asked about his arm strength. It was always a point of curiosity because Elway to this day is considered to have the strongest arm in NFL history. The Nolan Ryan of NFL quarterbacks. "I thought Favre did," Elway said of the Packers quarterback.

"But, yeah, without a doubt, I was very proud of it. I had a lot of confidence in my arm. I always had it. When I was young, I threw everything: dirt clods, snowballs. Walking home from school, light poles, cars."

Cars? "My mom said, 'John, if you get caught and you get put in jail, I'm not coming to get you.'" *Windows?* "Never broke any windows," he said.

What did the Broncos have in Elway in his final two years of 1997 and 1998? "We had a Super Bowl-winning, Super Bowl MVP quarterback is what we had," said starting receiver Ed McCaffrey. "If you look at his stats those last couple years, his stats were pretty darn good, and that was back in the day where there were no rules to protect the quarterback. Quarterbacks could get body slammed, thrown to the ground, hit high, hit low. It didn't matter. So he was a tough dude, man. He didn't lose any arm strength whatsoever. You can talk to him about how he felt, but I'm telling you I've got two dislocated ring fingers to prove he could throw the ball with the same velocity. Now maybe he didn't feel as fast as when he was first in the league, but he ran for touchdowns in both of our Super Bowls. So he could still move. And obviously you remember the Helicopter play, right?"

Rod Smith was the other starting receiver in 1997–98. What did Smith think of Elway's arm strength in the final years of his career? "The cool part about that question: John and I had that conversation after we retired," Smith said. "This is when the Broncos had Teddy Bridgewater and Drew Lock. We were watching practice. And Drew threw hard like John did most of his career. Teddy Bridgewater threw soft like John sometimes did in his later days. John could still throw the ball hard at the end, but he didn't have to. I think it was a rep where Drew threw it a little late, but he threw hard and got it to the hole. Teddy came in and threw it early, threw it soft, and it was a catchable ball that was thrown to the same hole. And John said, 'As you get older and you understand the game more, you don't have to throw these bullets. Once you understand timing, you can pace the ball where you need it.' I had five solid years with John, the last five years of his career, and he threw it as hard as he needed to throw it because he had so many reps, he knew so much about the position of defenders that he would throw you open."

Elway was back for one more season. T.D. was at his best. Bowlen was about to get a new stadium. Shanahan was intent on fine-tuning the Broncos' machine into the best team Denver had ever seen. As the defending champions, it wasn't supposed to be as easy as they made it look.

"In '98 that's when there's pressure," Broncos running back and returner Vaughn Hebron told 9NEWS at the 25-year reunion of the 1998 Super Bowl team. "You're at the mountaintop. It's always hard to stay on the mountaintop.

So everybody to a man took that personally. We knew what it was going to be. We knew we were going to be marked by everybody. We weren't going to sneak up on anybody. So we took that type of attitude and that approach into the season and, when we went 13–0, showed it."

Here's a game-by-game look at how the 1998 Broncos dominated the NFL.

Game One

September 7—Broncos 27, New England Patriots 21 at Mile High Stadium

Earlier on this Labor Day Monday, the St. Louis Cardinals' Mark McGwire hit his 61st home run to tie Roger Maris' single-season record. That Monday night John Elway showed a primetime audience he could still play at an elite level as he threw darts to various parts of the field in a 22-of-34, 257-yard performance. He threw a first-quarter touchdown pass to Shannon Sharpe, and Terrell Davis ran for two touchdowns—both of which he surprisingly celebrated with his trademark Mile High Salute.

Surprising because Davis had said the salute would be retired along with left tackle Gary Zimmerman, who this time hung 'em up for good because of acute shoulder pain from all those years of football collisions. But before the game, Davis put the Mile High Salute to a teammate vote, and the salute stayed. Otherwise, Davis only rushed for 75 yards off 22 carries, a 3.4-yard average that created no early hint that a 2,000-yard season was upon him. That sign would come in Week Two.

Game Two

September 13—Broncos 42, Dallas Cowboys 23 at Mile High Stadium

On back-to-back plays in the first quarter, Terrell Davis rushed 63 yards for a touchdown and 59 yards for a touchdown to turn a 7–7 tie into a 21–7 Broncos advantage. Davis had 154 yards and the two touchdowns on just 12 carries at halftime, and John Elway reached the intermission 11-of-13 for 217 yards and had two touchdowns to Shannon Sharpe. The Denver Broncos were up 35–17 at the break, scoring five touchdowns on their first five drives, and cruised in from there.

Except for Elway. Early in the fourth quarter, the 38 year old pulled his hamstring on a boot throw to Ed McCaffery for seven yards. Bubby Brister came in and threw one pass to Sharpe for 38 yards, setting up first and goal. Davis took it from there for his third touchdown. Brister didn't throw another pass the rest of the game. He didn't need to as Davis finished with 191 yards rushing. Cowboys quarterback Troy Aikman, a three-time Super Bowl winner earlier in the 1990s decade, suffered a fractured clavicle in the game.

Game Three

September 20—Broncos 34, Oakland Raiders 17 at Network Associates Coliseum

Questionable to play because of his sore hamstring, John Elway did start and threw a touchdown pass to Ed McCaffrey on the Denver Broncos' second series to take a 7–0 lead. It was 7–3 Broncos with 8:15 remaining in the second quarter when Elway rolled right and completed a first-down pass to Shannon Sharpe to the Oakland 19-yard line. But again Elway came up lame, clutching his right hamstring.

Again, Bubby Brister came in, but this time his first pass was intercepted by Raiders safety Eric Turner, who returned it 94 yards for a touchdown. The Raiders were up 10–7, and Elway was done for the game. "I kind of got mad at Mike [Shanahan] because I pulled a hamstring against the Cowboys on a boot," Elway recalled in November 2023. "So I came out, and then the next week, we went to Oakland. It was nip and tuck whether I'd go, and I said, 'Let me give it a shot.' And I thought Mike would protect me, but he called the boot again, and I do it again, got a little mad at Mike for that."

Both times Elway's hammy went on a play called Fake 19 Toss. "I do need to be smarter about my play selection, especially when John is in there." Shanahan admitted after the game.

No worries. Brister bounced back to throw two touchdown passes, and the Broncos intercepted Raiders quarterback

Jeff George three times. Ray Crockett had two of them and returned one 80 yards for a touchdown. Terrell Davis had a workmanlike 104 yards rushing off 28 carries.

Game Four

September 27—Broncos 38, Washington Redskins 16 at Jack Kent Cooke Stadium

In a peculiar move, John Elway dressed but didn't play. He was unable to play because of the aggravated hamstring. What was peculiar was that he dressed. Basically, the Denver Broncos had a backup quarterback who couldn't come in if Bubby Brister got hurt. The third-string quarterback, third-round rookie Brian Griese, was inactive. "We went to Washington. We're in the hotel, and Mike [Shanahan] calls me to his room," Elway recalled. "He said, 'John, I want you to dress tomorrow.' I said, 'Mike, don't you think if I could go, I would go?' In his defense he said, 'I don't want you to go. I'm going to start Bubby, but I want you to dress because I want them thinking you're going to play.'"

As we learned from Terrell Davis' migraine episode in Super Bowl XXXII, Shanahan loved to use his stars as decoys. Elway did dress, but he was one of two activated players who didn't play. "Which I understood," Elway said.

Rod Smith, the Broncos' top receiver who played quarterback in high school and his first year or two in college, would have been the emergency quarterback if Brister twisted an ankle. Luckily, Smith wasn't needed at quarterback. Brister threw touchdown passes of 19 yards to Ed McCaffrey and 14 yards to fullback Howard Griffith.

Darrien Gordon had a 55-yard pick-six off Trent Green to give Denver a 17–0, second-quarter lead, and Davis exploded for a 42-yard touchdown run to cap the opening series of the second half. Davis had 119 yards on 21 carries, giving him 489 rushing yards at the quarter-pole—just shy of a 2,000-yard pace. "The rest of the league should be wary," Gordon said. "We're the best team in football right now."

Game Five

October 4—Broncos 41, Philadelphia Eagles 16 at Mile High Stadium

Again, John Elway dressed but didn't play. But this time Mike Shanahan minimized his risk by also dressing Brian Griese, who did make his NFL debut by mopping up the fourth quarter in a blowout win. Bubby Brister was terrific, throwing four touchdown passes to the right guys—two to Rod Smith, one each to Shannon Sharpe and Ed McCaffrey. It was 28–0 Denver Broncos after the first quarter and 41–2 with five minutes left in the third quarter, at which point Shanahan pulled Brister and Terrell Davis, who was sensational with 168 yards rushing and two touchdowns off

20 carries. "Coach Shanahan put together a heck of a team," Brister said at the 1997 Super Bowl reunion. "And I was just glad to be a part of it,"

The Philadelphia Eagles were miserable, going 3–13 with Ray Rhodes as their coach and Bobby Hoying—who finished the season with zero touchdown passes and nine interceptions—as their first starting quarterback. And they were outrushed by the Broncos 132 to minus-1 in the first quarter.

Their talent level was quite a contrast to Denver's. "The MVPs are our offensive line and Terrell Davis," Sharpe told *The Denver Post*. "Bubby was all happy he threw four touchdown passes? Hey, I told him I could have thrown three myself against that team. It wasn't like we were playing the '85 Bears or something."

Game Six
October 11—Broncos 21, Seattle Seahawks 16 at the Kingdome

John Elway returned in style, throwing a 50-yard touchdown pass to Rod Smith and 19-yard score to Shannon Sharpe in the first quarter for a 14–0 lead. It was a struggle from there as Elway threw a pick-six to start the second quarter and another interception in his next possession.

At that point, Mike Shanahan had a nice alternative game plan: he handed play-calling duties over to offensive coordinator Gary Kubiak, who came up with a series of plays that amounted to Terrell Davis left (for five yards), Davis left (for nine yards), Davis left (for five yards), and Davis left (to finish the fourth quarter drive with a two-yard touchdown).

The running back carried 30 times for 208 yards. The Seattle Seahawks rallied behind backup quarterback John Friesz, who replaced Warren Moon in the fourth quarter. Friesz threw a 50-yard touchdown pass to former Denver Broncos receiver Mike Pritchard early in the quarter, then moved the Seahawks to the Denver 28-yard line at the two-minute warning. But on third and 9, Friesz was picked off over the middle by backup linebacker Glenn Cadrez, and the Broncos held on.

The 5–0 Minnesota Vikings had a bye. That left the Broncos as the NFL's only 6–0 team, putting the 1972 Miami Dolphins on alert.

Game Seven
October 25—Broncos 37, Jacksonville Jaguars 24 at Mile High Stadium

The Jacksonville Jaguars under coach Tom Coughlin started the season 5–0 and were coming off a one-point loss at Buffalo. So the Denver Broncos' first game after the bye week was highly anticipated. Given Jacksonville's history as Bronco villains, it would have been highly anticipated even if Jacksonville was 1–5 coming in.

This game wasn't all that competitive. The Broncos were up 27–10 at halftime as John Elway threw a 41-yard touchdown pass to Ed McCaffrey, Terrell Davis had two short touchdown runs, and Jason Elam kicked two field goals, including a 63-yarder at the halftime buzzer to tie Tom Dempsey's 28-year record. Dempsey's 63-yard field goal would be tied multiple times later, but Elam was the first, and his boot created considerable buzz among the 75,217 fans in the stands and the Broncos players on the field. Davis rushed for 136 yards to tie an NFL record shared by Jim Brown and O.J. Simpson by surpassing 1,000 yards rushing after just seven games.

Game Eight

November 1—Broncos 33, Cincinnati Bengals 26 at Cinergy Field

The Cincinnati Bengals came in with a 2–5 record, but they gave the mistake-prone Denver Broncos a scare. It was only 13–12 Broncos after three quarters, then came a wild fourth quarter in which Cincinnati quarterback Neil O'Donnell threw one touchdown pass to put the Bengals up 18–13 with 12 minutes remaining and another with 2:54 left to tie the game at 26.

But Vaughn Hebron returned a kickoff 38 yards to the Denver 47, and on the first play of the ensuing drive, John

Elway hit Ed McCaffrey for 30 yards to the Bengals' 23 at the two-minute warning. Elway hit McCaffrey again to set up first and goal at the 6, and Terrell Davis took it in from there with 1:03 remaining. It was Elway's 46th fourth quarter, game-saving drive.

Alfred Williams, the former Bengals defender, sacked O'Donnell on the first play of the final series to secure Denver's win. The T.D. 2,000-yard watch was officially on. "What helped it out was the fact we were winning," Davis said as he looked back at his signature season in November 2023. "It would have been a different conversation had we not been successful and 2,000 was the goal. I'm not a stats guy. I just thank God that I was able to do my job, and this came along as a bonus. The first time it became—*wait a minute*—was halfway through the season. I believe I had 1,000 yards after eight games. I think that's when you start thinking, *What if?*"

He actually had 1,001 yards after seven games and 1,150 after eight games—a pace for 2,300, which would have zipped past Eric Dickerson's record of 2,105.

Two days after they beat the Bengals, the Broncos were 8–0, and voters approved an extension of the 0.1 percent Coors Field tax to fund a new stadium for the Broncos and owner Pat Bowlen. "We were a fine-tuned machine," Davis said. "It was fun. It was no stress. My focus was not on two grand. My focus was on winning. And it was on putting us back on playoff mode. What was our best position? If we could get the playoffs to come through Mile High, we preferred that. It was beautiful. When you're halfway through the season and you're not thinking about playoffs, you're thinking about what seed you want. That's a beautiful thing."

Game Nine

October 25—Broncos 27, San Diego Chargers 10 at Mile High Stadium

John Elway came into this game needing only 42 yards to join Dan Marino as the only players in NFL history to throw for 50,000 career yards. He wouldn't get there in this game. Unbeknownst to the public leading up to the San Diego Chargers game, Elway suffered a rib injury during the previous week's win against the Cincinnati Bengals. He finished that game, but once the adrenaline wore off, he was in pain. "We were in Cincinnati that year, and I fell on the ball," Elway recalled. "I fumbled the snap on the 1. So I just fell on it, and they all jumped on me, and I could feel my chest go *creak*. Rib cartilage. That whole week I couldn't take a deep breath. My cadence was weak. We played the Chargers the next week, and I take a [pain-killing] shot."

He aggravated his ribs during pregame warmups, and Bubby Brister started and played the first series, throwing an interception. Elway jogged out for the second series to thunderous applause from the sellout crowd, but after a 12-yard completion to Rod Smith, he winced through an incompletion and then was clobbered by the great Chargers linebacker Junior Seau for a nine-yard sack. "They kept giving me shots, and I kept going. I started to bleed. I said, 'You don't have it yet.' [Head trainer Steve Antonopulos] goes, 'I've got bad news. No. 1, we're at the legal limit. I can't give you anymore. And No. 2, we're out anyway.' So I go out the next series, and we bust a protection, and Junior Seau comes and hits me right here," said Elway as he pointed to the bridge of his nose between the eyes. He went cross-eyed for effect. "I'm going down, going, 'Oohhh, that's going to hurt.'"

It was another hint for Elway that his battered body didn't have many hits left. "And that's the thing: you just don't heal as fast," he said. "I felt like I was breaking down a little bit."

So the Broncos played their division rival Chargers without Elway and with Terrell Davis only rushing for 69 yards, a season-low at the time, on 20 carries. And the Broncos were still up 27–0 after the third quarter. Once Brister realized he was the quarterback for the day, he settled in. He completed 20-of-33 passes for 229 yards and touchdowns to Ed McCaffrey, who had nine catches for 133 yards on the day, and Davis, who had the four-yard scoring reception plus a 24-yard run. The Mile High crowd started chanting, "ED-DIE! ED-DIE!"

The Denver Broncos were a juggernaut. With people starting to whisper about Elway growing old, Brister was 3–0 in his three starts, 4–0 as a practical matter, and that was from a veteran quarterback who was 1–5 as a starter in three previous years. "I feel like I'm more 26 than 36," Brister said.

Game 10

November 16—Broncos 30, Kansas City Chiefs 7 at Arrowhead Stadium

Another dominant Monday night performance by the juggernaut 1998 Denver Broncos, this was the game where Broncos tight end Shannon Sharpe got under the skin of Kansas City Chiefs star outside linebacker Derrick Thomas.

Bubby Brister again started in place of the injured John Elway, and on the first series, the backup quarterback ran for a 38-yard touchdown. On the second series, Davis ran for a 41-yard touchdown. The Broncos were up 14–0. With eight minutes remaining in the first quarter before a Monday night audience, the game was already over. But the Chiefs managed to turn their franchise into several more shades of red in the fourth quarter. With 7:36 remaining the Broncos led 23–7 when they took the ball at their own 20. First, Chiefs defensive tackle Chester McGlockton was flagged for unnecessary roughness. Then Thomas was flagged three times—the first for clobbering Brister in the helmet, the next two for purposely grabbing Sharpe's face mask.

It seems Sharpe, who lined up across from Thomas, started reciting the phone number of Thomas' girlfriend. All those penalty yards eased the Broncos down the field for an 80-yard drive that Derek Loville capped with a two-yard touchdown run. Loville spelled Davis late in the third quarter after Davis was knocked dizzy. At least that's how it was described in the papers. Today it would have been called a concussion. Before he left, Davis had already rushed for 111 yards on just 18 carries.

Brister had thrown for 180 yards and rushed for 47 to finish the season officially 4–0 as a starter. Like the 1972 Miami Dolphins, who went 17–0 with backup quarterback Earl Morrall winning 11 games as a starter, the Broncos were 4–0 with Brister, who essentially had a 5–0 record. The 1998 Broncos seemed every bit worthy of joining the '72 Dolphins in the history books.

Game 11

November 22—Broncos 40, Oakland Raiders 14 at Mile High Stadium

John Elway was back and was terrific, completing 17-of-25 for 197 yards—at long last he surpassed 50,000 career passing yards—and three touchdowns. Ed McCaffrey was out with a hamstring injury, but Rod Smith had six catches, including a 28-yard touchdown; Shannon Sharpe had a seven-yard touchdown catch; and Terrell Davis shook off the cobwebs to rush for 162 yards on 31 carries. Unlike so many of their other wins when they got up big early and coasted, the Denver Broncos only led 17–14 late in the third quarter, then poured it on with 23 unanswered points in the fourth quarter. *What, you thought Mike Shanahan was going to let off the gas against Al Davis' Raiders?*

Game 12

November 29—Broncos 31, San Diego Chargers 16 at Qualcomm Stadium

John Elway threw three interceptions in the second quarter, Terrell Davis was held to 74 yards rushing on 24 carries, and the Denver Broncos still clinched the AFC West Division title—with four games to go. "For a while there, we were playing one of our worst games," wide receiver Rod Smith told *The Denver Post*, "and they were playing one of their best."

And the Broncos still won by two touchdowns.

One reason is Elway also threw a season-most four touchdown passes. Ed McCaffrey returned in a big way as he caught touchdown passes of 15 and 37 yards from Elway in the first quarter. Smith had eight catches for 101 yards and a touchdown with seconds remaining in the first half to give Denver a 21–10 lead.

The biggest reason why the Broncos won was their defense intercepted five passes, including two by Darrien Gordon, who also recovered a fumble, off San Diego Chargers quarterback Craig Whelihan. The Broncos became the fourth team to start a season 12–0 and first since the '85 Chicago Bears.

Game 13

December 6—Broncos 35, Kansas City Chiefs 31 at Mile High Stadium

The strain of an undefeated record was beginning to show. The 5–7 Kansas City Chiefs led 14–0 early on two touchdown passes by Rich Gannon, 21–7 midway through the second quarter, and 31–21 midway through the fourth quarter as the Denver Broncos' home crowd of 74,962 grew anxious.

But then John Elway did it again—for one final time in the fourth quarter. After another big kickoff return by Vaughn Hebron, the Broncos took over at their 46 down 31–21 with 8:25 remaining. Elway hit Willie Green for a 50-yard completion to set up first and goal at the 1. Terrell Davis scored from there.

Then after Gannon threw three straight incompletions for a three-and-out, the Broncos' Darrien Gordon had a nice punt return to the 50, where Elway took over with 6:13 remaining. Elway completed passes of 12 yards to Davis and 24 yards to Shannon Sharpe for a touchdown with 3:34 remaining, and the Broncos held on for win No. 13. It was Sharpe's only catch of the game.

Elway threw for 400 yards for just the second time in his career. He also picked up his 47th—and final—fourth-quarter, game-saving drive. "It's been a long time since we have been in a game as close as this," Elway said at his postgame press conference. "It was back and forth all day. It was fun. It felt like the old days."

The Dan Reeves days. Davis was held in check for a second consecutive game with 88 yards on 24 carries. That put him at 1,654 yards, meaning he would need 346 yards with three games remaining—or a hardly certain 115.3 per game.

The Broncos tied an NFL record with their 18th consecutive victory going back to 1997.

"The crown is getting heavier," Denver defensive end Neil Smith told *The Denver Post*.

"The closer you get to the record," Broncos cornerback Ray Crockett said, "the more everyone wants to be the team that ends your streak."

Game 14

December 13—New York Giants 20, Broncos 16 at Giants Stadium

The 1996–98 Denver Broncos just missed going down as arguably the greatest team in NFL history. Just missed a threepeat. Just missed an undefeated season. Not playing their best for a third week in a row, the Broncos this time fell. The New York Giants were just 5–8 coming in, but they were at home, and their focus was on becoming the team that prevented the Broncos from a perfect season.

The Giants were up 10–6 at halftime thanks to a Kent Graham touchdown pass to Tiki Barber, and it was 13–9 Giants in the fourth quarter. But with four minutes remaining, Terrell Davis ran for a 27-yard touchdown, and the Broncos were up 16–13. But on third and 10 with 57 seconds left, Graham threw a 37-yard touchdown to Amani Toomer in the right corner of the end zone. Toomer beat reserve nickelback Tito Paul on the play. John Elway had just 48 seconds to drive from his own 42 for a go-ahead touchdown. Completions of 17 yards to Rod Smith and 20 yards to Willie Green got the Broncos to the Giants' 30-yard line. But time ran out—much to the delight of the '72 Miami Dolphins. "Speaking for myself, I'm happy as hell that's off my back," Broncos defensive tackle Keith Traylor told *The Denver Post*. "We're still champions, and champions don't ever like to lose. It hurts. But for myself, it was wearing me down. I was tired of hearing it. Everywhere I went, people would ask, 'You guys going undefeated?' And I always told them, 'I…don't…know.' I just want to win the Super Bowl."

Game 15

December 21—Miami Dolphins 31, Broncos 21 at Pro Player Stadium

Monday Night Football just missed getting what it wanted. It wanted a 14–0 Denver Broncos team to take on the Miami Dolphins at Pro Player Stadium—with all the 1972 Dolphins' alumni watching from the sideline. That's just what the 12–0 Chicago Bears had to endure in 1985. The Bears' great 46 defense got torched by Dan Marino that night in a 38–24 loss in Miami—Chicago's only loss in an otherwise dominant Super Bowl Shuffle-winning season.

Monday Night Football didn't quite get the same hype from a Broncos–Dolphins matchup 14 years later. "It didn't matter," John Elway said in November 2023.

The pressure of 16–0 was gone but so was the motivation. Elway and Terrell Davis each had by far their worst performances of the season. Bothered by a sore groin, Elway was 13-of-36 with no touchdowns and two interceptions. Davis, who suffered bruised ribs in the first quarter, only rushed for 29 yards on 16 carries.

His 2,000-yard goal was all but cooked as he was 170 yards short with but a meaningless season finale against the Seattle Seahawks left. "The Miami game I thought was the deal breaker," Davis said in *Mile High Magic: The 25 Greatest Moments in Denver Broncos History*. "I didn't think I was going to get 2,000 yards. We had already clinched home-field advantage. There was no need for us to really play that [final] game, and I didn't think the coaches would keep me in long enough to get 2,000 yards. So I had kissed the 2,000-yard campaign goodbye. I remember sitting on the flight going back home. I was next to Derek Loville, and we were looking at the stat sheet, and he looks at me and says, 'Man, you could have had 2,000 yards.' I said, 'Yep, you're right. It's gone now.'"

It was the Dolphins who were motivated as they clinched a playoff spot with the win. In one of the few head-to-head matchups between the two best of the great quarterback draft class of 1983, Marino sliced up the listless Denver defense for 355 yards passing and four touchdowns. To Marino's credit he was humble in victory when asked if the win was more satisfying because it was against Elway, the No. 1 overall selection in the 1983 draft. "It's more satisfying because the Dolphins won, and we're in the playoffs," said Marino, who was drafted second-to-last at No. 27 in that same 1983 draft. "John's a special player and the best quarterback I've ever seen. To play against him for a second time was fun. But the more important thing was winning the game."

The whipping in South Florida would have been worse if not for Vaughn Hebron's 95-yard kickoff return for a touchdown midway through the fourth quarter. It was the Broncos' first kickoff return for a touchdown since Randy Montgomery did so in 1972.

Game 16

December 27—Broncos 28, Seattle Seahawks 21 at Mile High Stadium

Terrell Davis did it. He thought he had no chance, but he did it. Against all odds, Davis rushed for 178 yards on 29 carries to break the 2,000-yard barrier with eight yards and eight minutes and 52 seconds to spare. At that point Mike Shanahan called timeout, and T.D. was replaced by Derek Loville to thunderous applause from the crowd of 74,057.

Clearly, Shanahan went out of his way to get Davis the 2,000 yards. *Twenty-nine carries in a meaningless final game?* "Jacksonville," John Elway said in 2023. "I think that game changed Mike's mentality because that '98 year we finished against Seattle and we played the whole game."

In 1996 Elway and T.D. played sparingly in two of the final three regular-season games, and the Denver Broncos got upset in their first playoff game. But in this 1998 regular-season finale against the Seattle Seahawks, Elway threw for 338 yards and four touchdowns—two to tight end Shannon Sharpe, one to Rod Smith, who was astounding with nine catches for 158 yards—and the other to Davis.

More importantly, the Broncos finished the regular season on a high note, winning to post a 14–2 record to again earn the No. 1 AFC playoff seed and a first-round bye. This time, unlike 1996, the Broncos would take advantage. "Now the funny thing—and I still tell this story—if I would have told you that we had an all-players meeting at 13–2, you'd be like, 'That's crazy,'" Vaughn Hebron said at the 1998 Super Bowl reunion in September 2023. "But the record is always about when the record occurred. If we would have lost the first two games and won 13 straight, we don't have that meeting. But we won 13 straight and then lost two in a row. And we had an all-players meeting, and John was like, 'The playoffs start now.' And the rest is history."

By virtue of his historical 2,008-yard rushing season, Davis was the NFL's Most Valuable Player. He garnered 25 of the possible 47 first-place votes. Minnesota Vikings quarterback Randall Cunningham, who went 13–1 in Minnesota's 15–1 season, received 14 first-place votes. Atlanta Falcons running back Jamal Anderson, who nearly matched T.D. by gaining 1,846 yards for coach Dan Reeves, and Vikings receiver Randy Moss, an incredible rookie who led the NFL with 17 touchdown catches, each had four first-place votes.

Looking back 26 years later, Davis issued most of the credit of his and the Broncos' success in the late 1990s to his head coach and offensive genius, Shanahan. "I loved the way Mike coached," Davis said. "I can't say enough about his coaching style and how he fit me as a player. He was very demanding. But what I loved about him being demanding was: Mike was going to give you everything. The trade-off was, 'I'm going to give you everything, but I'm going to demand from you everything.' Fair. He's going to be fair and he's going to push you. That's the way I like to be coached. And the other thing is: I always wanted to know why. Why are we going to do X, Y, and Z? Mike would tell us the why. And then he wasn't afraid to take chances. Like when he got rid of Anthony Miller, he got rid of Michael Dean Perry, these are really good players. You don't get rid of Pro Bowlers for a dude who was on the practice squad [Smith]. You don't do that, but Mike did. It's pruning. It's like taking that rose bush and cutting it. You don't want to cut it, but when you do, you open some light for some younger pieces. There was definitely some merit in sometimes you have to take steps backward to go forward. Coaches see players every day. They have the advantage of seeing players not only on the practice field but the locker room. They have access to players all the time.

"Even coaching now, the public perception may be one thing about a player, but they don't know everything about a player. They don't know why a certain player isn't playing. He may have something that drives me crazy as a coach. I can't trust him to put him in a game. He's a talent. But Mike would say, 'You may not see it,' or he wasn't afraid to be wrong. Let's say he did it for Rod, and Rod didn't turn out. It was bold, man. I started my first career NFL game. I'm a sixth-round draft pick. He didn't bring me in slowly. No, my first NFL game was a start. Come on now." The Broncos were three postseason games away from going back-to-back. As they did all season, the Broncos would dominate. And Elway would get the perfect ending.

CHAPTER FIFTEEN

GOING OUT ON TOP

J ohn Elway would come in with his adversary Dan Reeves. And Elway would go out against his adversary Reeves. You couldn't make it up. Okay, so that might be a bit of an exaggeration. It's way too strong to call Reeves an adversary during Elway's NFL formative years. Reeves was Elway's head coach for 10 years, and together the Denver Broncos went 98–60 in the regular season—an average of 10–6—with three Super Bowl appearances and four AFC Championship Games. Not everything has a Hallmark ring to work.

Did Reeves' offense stifle Elway's immense talent? Given the context of four more years with Mike Shanahan as head coach, Elway and everyone else who followed the Broncos would have to say, yes, to some extent Reeves did. Except for the fourth quarter, of course, when Reeves had to turn Elway loose in the name of victory. But let there be no doubt there was extreme tension in the final years of Reeves and Elway/Shanahan with the Broncos. Say the final three (1990–92) seasons. And that tension did not relax. It carried on—if strained below the surface—for at least six more years.

Proof was Reeves' first Super Bowl XXXIII press conference as head coach of the Atlanta Falcons. To support the adage there are two sides to every story, each of the three parties were successful without the other. The third party in this long-held grudge being Shanahan, whom Reeves fired after the 1991 season.

Shanahan did pretty well in his first five seasons when he had control. He first moved on to become the San Francisco 49ers offensive coordinator. The 49ers led the NFL in scoring all three years Shanahan was masterminding their offense and crushed all comers on their way to winning the Super Bowl after the 1994 season.

Shanahan then became head coach of the Broncos, who were the defending Super Bowl champions heading into their quest to repeat against Reeves' Falcons in XXXIII. Elway flourished without Reeves, too. In his first season without Reeves, Elway had his first and only 4,000-yard passing season with Jim Fassel as his offensive coordinator. Elway's three highest number of single-season touchdown passes came in his first three seasons running Shanahan's system, and he posted three of his top four passer ratings under Shanahan. And Elway was 35–8 in his last three seasons under Shanahan. Oh, and by the way, Elway had finally won the Big One in 1997.

But wait. Reeves did fine, too. The first year after Reeves was fired by Pat Bowlen, he turned around the New York

Giants from 6–10 the year before he arrived to 11–5 with a first-round playoff win in his first season there in 1993. Reeves then became head coach of the Falcons in 1997, replacing June Jones who was 3–13 in 1996. It took Reeves just two years to transform the Falcons into a 14–2 NFC West champion (the league's realignment correction wouldn't come until 2002) who shocked the 15–1 Minnesota Vikings in the NFC Championship Game.

The Vikings were so dominant in 1998 that they would have been two-point favorites against the Broncos in Super Bowl XXXIII. Their superior set of weapons led by Randy Moss, Cris Carter, Robert Smith, and Randall Cunningham would have been a difficult matchup for the Broncos. Against the Falcons, whose quarterback was journeyman Chris Chandler, the Broncos were seven-and-a-half point favorites.

Jason Elam kicked off the AFC Championship Game against the New York Jets at 2:17 PM MST Sunday, January 17. Morten Andersen kicked an overtime field goal to give Reeves' Falcons a shocking, 30–27 upset win against the Vikings at 2:18 PM MST the same day. So the Broncos' AFC Championship Game had started before the Broncos knew the Falcons had upset the Vikings.

In the halftime locker room, even though his team was struggling, Shanahan was pleased to hear the Falcons had won. Not because he wanted vindication against Reeves, though maybe a little. It's just Shanahan felt his Broncos matched up better against the Falcons. He must have expressed his preference to owner Pat Bowlen, who later spilled to a local newspaper the Broncos were happy to be facing the Falcons— and not the Vikings—in the Super Bowl. "The staff around here tells me we match up better against the Falcons than we do against the Vikings," Bowlen said with incredulous candor to *The Denver Post* after the Broncos rallied to defeat the Jets in the AFC Championship Game. "We don't match up against guys who are 6'6" with 100-inch vertical leaps. We don't match up against basketball players playing football because that's what it looked like sometimes when Randall Cunningham was lobbing those passes out there, and these guys were going up there and slam dunking it. Defensively, we would rather play the Falcons—not that we think that they're any less of a football team. It's just a better matchup for us."

Holy Howard Cosell, Pat Bowlen. Tell it like it is. The Vikings and Broncos might have been a better matchup of dominant teams, but there was a far greater dramatic storyline to The Big Game pitting Reeves against Elway/Shanahan. And that drama was immediately sparked by Reeves in the days after the conference championship games.

The Denver Post sent Jim Armstrong, an excellent sports-writer known for his breezy, conversational touch, to the Falcons' practice facility in Suwanee, Georgia, to cover Reeves.

On Wednesday, January 20, Reeves held his first press conference since his team shocked the Vikings. After a few questions
were asked by the local Atlanta reporters, Armstrong, who was
a Broncos beat reporter for a time during the Reeves' era in
Denver, asked Reeves what he thought of the job Shanahan
had done as his assistant coach. About 20 minutes later, Reeves
was done answering the question. Let's just say Reeves tossed
more brickbats than bouquets. "I didn't think he had my best
interests in mind at the time," Reeves said. "If John Elway had
a problem with me and you're coaching that position, why did
I not know that prior to reading it in the paper? If you were
the position coach and you're that close to the quarterback,
why didn't I know that? 'Hey, this is something you ought to
sit down and talk about, that this is a problem.'"

Reeves was referring to the 1990 column written in
The Denver Post by the late Hall of Fame sportswriter Dick
Connor to whom Elway trusted to air his grievances in the
midst of a 5–11 season—the only losing record in the 10-year
Reeves/Elway term. In the Connor piece, Elway said he and
Reeves no longer communicated and that their relationship
was "the worst."

Reeves reacted by going into Shanahan's offensive coordinator office and threw the newspaper down on his desk.
"The only thing that you could have a feeling that maybe John
was upset with were things you say at a coaches' meeting,"

Reeves said. "You say things in a coaches' meeting as far as critiquing the play of someone that you would never say to the player. If John ever got any bad feelings about something I said, it never was done publicly. It had to be something from a staff meeting that you said. Now does that mean Mike did it? You've got a lot of people on your staff. These are things that in your mind…I have no proof of them, but I did what I thought was best for our football team."

That meant firing Shanahan after the 1991 season when the Broncos went 12–4 and lost to the Buffalo Bills in the AFC Championship Game. Reeves also claimed—then and during that Suwanee press conference—Shanahan and Elway scripted plays behind his back. Asked if he blamed Shanahan or Elway for his firing, Reeves said, "In my mind Mike Shanahan would have been hired [as head coach] when I was fired. But there was too much public opinion that would have made it almost impossible for him to do it. I think two years later was a much better situation. Do I have proof of that? I have no proof of that. But in my mind, that's what I think."

Reeves later added: "I don't know that I'll ever get over the full situation. I don't know that Mike will ever get over that—what it caused his wife and his children. Same thing with me. It caused a lot of pain for my wife and my children. It's something that won't ever go away. It's going to be there."

Goodness. Maybe next time, Dan, tell us how you really feel.

Shanahan was livid at Reeves' Super Bowl-opening salvos, particularly the claims of insubordination. It was no secret Bowlen wanted Shanahan to succeed Reeves as head coach in 1993. But Shanahan turned the offer down in large part because Bowlen couldn't guarantee in writing certain conditions Shanahan had asked for—conditions showed to him by the 49ers, a proven championship franchise.

But Reeves' claim that Shanahan ratted him out caused Shanahan's face to boil red. "I thought I did a great job of keeping that relationship intact for seven years," Shanahan told *The Denver Post* when Reeves' comments were relayed. "He came to me and was very upset about [the Connor column]. I said, 'What are you talking to me for? John said it. Go talk to John.' I went down to the weight room and got John and brought him up to Dan's office. I said, 'John, you tell Dan why you don't like him, and Dan, you tell John why you don't like him. I'm tired of being in the middle of this stuff.' So they both did."

Elway, too, was upset at hearing how Reeves brought back the play script complaint and also denied he and Shanahan kept it secret from their head coach. It took a couple days for Reeves to comprehend the furor his comments created. When he and his Falcons arrived Sunday, January 24 in Miami, where Super Bowl XXXIII would be played, the first thing he did was use his press conference to apologize for letting everyone know the grudge had yet to be buried years later. "There's an awful lot of wounds by a lot of people," Reeves said. "I caused some of it in my experience at Denver. And the only thing I know that cures wounds is time. And I apologize for the opening of the wounds last week because I don't think anything was accomplished by it. It doesn't change anything...I should be smart enough. I've been in this business 18, 19 years. I've been a head coach, and when you try to cooperate and people keep asking the same question, you know they're going to make a lot more out of it than what you thought. I apologize to anybody who was hurt."

At the time the Falcons brushed these comments aside. "You're talking about old stuff that we don't give credence to," said Falcons safety Eugene Robinson. "It has no bearing on what you're going to do."

As it turned out, Robinson would do something on the eve of the Super Bowl that would have far greater significance on how the game would play out. The drama to Super Bowl XXXIII, you see, wasn't restricted to the Reeves–Elway/Shanahan feud. There was also the buzz about Elway retiring after the game that kept the football world guessing throughout the week. And Robinson received the Bart Starr Man of the Year Award on the Saturday morning before the Super

Bowl—only to get busted in a prostitution ring a few hours later in a story that was so over-the-top salacious, Hollywood couldn't make it up. But before reaching a Super Bowl replete with storylines, here's how the Broncos rolled through the playoffs.

AFC divisional playoff game
January 9—Broncos 38, Miami Dolphins 3 at Mile High Stadium

The morning of the game, the NFL announced Denver Broncos running back Terrell Davis as the Associated Press' 1998 NFL Most Valuable Player. It didn't go to his head. A few hours later, Davis rushed for 199 yards and two touchdowns off a relatively modest 21 carries.

"I didn't think about it going into this game," David said. "I'm not going to walk out onto the field and think just because I'm the MVP that good things are going to happen."

The same Miami Dolphins that held Davis to 29 yards on 15 carries and beat the Broncos 31–21 in Miami just three weeks earlier discovered the Broncos were a different team when the game had something at stake. "People had been jumping off the bandwagon," John Elway said. "The doubters had been coming from everywhere."

Not really, but since the beginning of time—at least since David used his slingshot to hit Goliath right between the eyes—nothing has motivated a player more than the "people said I couldn't do it" card.

The 35-point drubbing was the largest margin of victory in Broncos postseason history, a record that stands 25 years later. Late in the first quarter with the Broncos up 14–0 on T.D.'s two touchdown runs, the sellout crowd of 75,729 (only 231 no-shows) began serenading Dolphins head coach Jimmy Johnson with "Jim-my! Jim-my!"

The Denver defense picked off Dan Marino twice while holding the Dolphins' running game to a meager 14 yards on 13 carries. Defensive end Neil Smith returned a fumble by Dolphins receiver Oronde Gadsden 79 yards down the left sideline for a touchdown. Meanwhile, the Broncos piled up 250 yards rushing thanks to Davis, and Elway was an efficient, stay-within-the-game-plan, 14-of-23 for 182 yards, including a 28-yard touchdown to Rod Smith early in the fourth quarter.

Elway had never previously beaten Marino or the Dolphins, but in his 16-year career, they only matched up twice before. The third time was indeed the charm and the one that counted—a playoff game for the right to advance to the AFC Championship Game—and Elway's Broncos won handily. "There will always be a rivalry built in there with the two of us," Elway said. "But this was about 46 other guys out there trying to win the game against 46 other guys."

AFC Championship Game
January 17—Broncos 23, New York Jets 10 at Mile High Stadium

This got a little scary. The Denver Broncos were down 3–0 in the first half as a strong wind made it near impossible for even the strong-armed John Elway to cut his passes through it. Elway was just 4-of-14 for 33 yards at the half. And he started 1-of-5 for seven yards in the second half. It became 10–0 four minutes into the second half after the New York Jets blocked a Tom Rouen punt to set up first and goal at the 1. Curtis Martin only had 14 yards rushing on 13 carries on the day, but he was able to finish off the one-play, one-yard drive. Incredulously, the powerhouse Broncos were in trouble.

Not for long.

A nice return by Vaughn Hebron on the ensuing kickoff gave Denver the ball at its 36-yard line. On the next play, Elway hit Ed McCaffrey on a post pattern—as the Jets safety bit on Rod Smith's underneath crossing route—for 47 yards to the Jets' 17. Two plays later Elway connected with fullback Howard Griffith for an 11-yard touchdown pass. It was 10–7.

Then came the play of the game. Jason Elam not only pooched the kickoff, but the ball also got caught up in the wind and landed at the Jets' 30. Jets return man Dave Meggett couldn't get it, forcing linebacker James Farrior to field it. He fumbled it almost immediately, and Broncos special teams standout Keith Burns recovered at the Jets' 31. That led to an Elam field goal and a 10–10 tie less than four minutes after the Jets took their 10–0 lead. Another Elam field goal two minutes later made it 13–10 Broncos.

And then a 36-yard punt return by Darrien Gordon gave the Broncos the ball at the Jets' 38 with 1:42 left in the third quarter. T.D. time. Terrell Davis carried the ball on three straight plays—for four yards, for three yards, and then on third and 3 for 31 yards and a touchdown. With 18 seconds left in the third quarter, the Broncos were in control, leading 20–10 after scoring 20 unanswered points in a 10-minute span.

Jets quarterback Vinny Testaverde threw two interceptions in the fourth quarter—part of the Jets' six turnovers on the day. It was not a day for great passing. Because of the strong wind, Elway was only 13-of-34 through the air, though he made his completions count for 173 yards. Shanahan had to rely on Davis, who had 167 yards off 32 carries. No back carries the ball as much today as Davis did from 1996 to 1998.

An elevated stage was rolled out for the Lamar Hunt AFC Championship Trophy presentation. "I LOVE YOU!" Elway shouted in the microphone to his 75,482 fans who gathered for what would be his last game at Mile High Stadium. It was a goodbye, if not yet official.

After the game Mike Shanahan and Elway were mag-nanimous in their comments toward Dan Reeves after his Atlanta Falcons upset the mighty Minnesota Vikings in the other conference championship game that day. "At times, we were best friends," Shanahan said of Reeves. "He's just done an incredible job."

"He's got them playing great, and Dan is a great football coach," Elway said.

The Broncos were willing to play nice so as to not dust up any motivational headlines for the Falcons. That changed three days later when *The Denver Post*'s Jim Armstrong asked Reeves about his time with Shanahan as his assistant and Elway as his quarterback. The emotional scabs were opened, and it was Reeves who ripped off the bandages. Super Bowl XXXIII featuring Reeves vs. Shanahan/Elway as the main storyline was on.

Super Bowl XXXIII

January 31—Broncos 34, Atlanta Falcons 19 at Pro Player Stadium

John Elway said before the season that he was 99.9 percent sure the upcoming season would be last. But then the 1998 season flipped to the January 1999 calendar and the post-season, and Elway started to fertilize that 0.1 percent. FOX Sports flashed an exclusive saying former San Francisco 49ers safety great Ronnie Lott, working for the network as an analyst, reported that if the Denver Broncos beat the Atlanta Falcons on Sunday, Elway might be tempted to play another year. "There'd be nothing better than to get two in a row and have to contemplate coming back for a third because nobody's ever done it three times in a row," Elway said. "So definitely, if we could get a win here, it would throw a little wrench into my thinking."

That same Monday before the Super Bowl, though, Mike Shanahan repeated what he had been saying: that he expected Super Bowl XXXIII to be Elway's final game with Denver. "My gut feeling is this will be his last football game," Shanahan said about Elway.

Meanwhile, Pat Bowlen said at the Super Bowl that when Elway did retire he was thinking about bringing him in as a minority owner. "It would be a natural," Bowlen said. "I know if John retires and he's thinking about his future, we'd sit down and talk about him owning a piece of the team. I know he doesn't want to be a coach. I think he wants to work here. But I think he probably wants to be a part of the ownership group. I'd welcome him."

On the eve of the Super Bowl, the Broncos got another piece of news that figured to help them and hurt the Falcons. On the morning before his Super Bowl encounter with the Broncos, Atlanta Falcons safety Eugene Robinson received the Bart Starr Award from Athletes in Action, the Christian-based group, for his high moral character.

Later that afternoon, Robinson relaxed poolside with his wife and son. Later that night—and about three hours before the Falcons' midnight curfew—Robinson allegedly drove to a South Beach area reputed for prostitutes. The Miami Police Department was setting up a solicitation sting, which landed 25 arrests, including Robinson, who, according to the police, offered $40 to an undercover agent for oral sex. "My lawyer has advised me not to talk about my arrest," Robinson read from a statement after the game. "I feel strongly in my heart that I'll be found innocent. But what I want to do now is apologize first of all to the Lord Jesus Christ and my wife and kids and finally to my teammates and the organization for the distractions I've caused. And I regret not adhering to the standard to the extent that I expect of myself."

From coach Dan Reeves to fellow defensive back Ray Buchanan to special-teams hero Tim Dwight, the Falcons said Robinson's arrest on Super Bowl eve was not a distraction, had no impact on their team's resounding defeat. But results suggested otherwise.

Pressed repeatedly about the charges against Robinson, Reeves finally pounded his fist on the podium and spoke passionately. "Any time you have somebody who does something like that, you're disappointed," Reeves said. "I don't know anybody who hasn't made a mistake in their lives. He's a member of our family, and we love him unconditionally... Nobody's more embarrassed about it than Eugene. I'm not going to crucify him over it."

Whether the arrest was to blame, Robinson appeared to play poorly. The play of the game came during the Broncos' first snap of their first possession late in the second quarter. Already leading 10–3, Elway faked a handoff to running back Terrell Davis. The defense froze. Elway looked downfield and saw Rod Smith in a dead sprint, converging on Robinson. Smith blew past the safety as his hands grabbed Elway's slightly underthrown pass. With the television cameras zeroing in on Smith's gallop, only No. 41—Robinson—was shown in futile pursuit. Though Denver wasn't able to put the Falcons away until early in the fourth quarter, the bomb to Smith left no doubt the biggest upset of Super Bowl XXXIII occurred the night before—when a man of seemingly impeccable character got busted.

Elway in his final game threw for 336 yards, including the 80-yard touchdown to Smith. He also ran for a three-yard touchdown with 11:20 left in the game to give the Broncos an insurmountable, 31–6 lead. Much too late, the Falcons scored two touchdowns—one on a 94-yard kickoff return by Dwight—to bring the final score to a misleading 34–19. It wasn't that close.

After all those miserable Super Bowls, Elway was the MVP on his fifth try. He won his last two, back-to-back. The second championship was never in doubt as the Broncos strategically took advantage of a potent Falcons defense. "It was a little bit different in the second Super Bowl because the way we were going to exploit the Atlanta Falcons was by keeping them in base," Broncos left guard Mark Schlereth said in October 2023. "They had a very exclusive and exotic blitz package. They led the league in sacks that year. They called themselves the Bomb Squad. And they had an unbelievably difficult blitz package. Their blitz package where they did their damage was in nickel situations, third and long, second and long. So what we ended up doing was we played that entire game in base. We never got out of two back. Terrell and Howard [Griffith] were in the whole time. Even in the passing game, those guys were in, so we threw against those guys not blitzing. So we exploited them with their linebackers trying to cover Shannon [Sharpe] until he got hurt. Then we were getting play-action, one-on-one with Rod Smith over the top."

The key play, of course, was an 80-yard touchdown to Smith. "It was an adjustment during the game," Elway said 25 years later. "We had run that play earlier, and I booted, and Eugene Robinson, the free safety, came up underneath on the comeback route. So he was way out of position underneath on the comeback route. And that's what we were talking about on the sidelines: let's do the same thing…Rod was on the weak side, and we blocked it and we said to Rod, 'Instead of running a comeback, run a post.' And sure enough he did it again and came underneath, and the safety bit."

The burnt safety was Robinson. "Anytime we ran a quarterback keep, their free safety was in charge of the tight end or receiver, whoever [Ed McCaffrey] was crossing in that 10-to-12-yard area, he was jumping," Shanahan said. "So I told Rod, 'Just be patient.' And he did a great job setting him up."

Robinson played in the last three Super Bowls, losing the last two. He was a Packers starting safety in Super Bowls XXXI and XXXII. Meanwhile, Super Bowls XXXII and XXXIII epitomized Smith. In the first Super Bowl, he didn't have a catch. In the second Super Bowl, he made the catch of the game, finishing with five receptions for 152 yards. An unselfish team player to win one, using his skill and underrated talent to win another. "Sometimes when I make a speech," Smith said in November 2023 a day before delivering a speech at a real estate conference, "if the timing is right, I ask a trivia question: 'What game in my starting career did I not have a catch?' There was one game I started I didn't have a catch. That was Super Bowl XXXII against the Packers. People say, 'Oh my God, what do you feel about that?' I tell them my ring is the same size as John Elway's. My ring is the same size as T.D's, same size as Shannon Sharpe's."

Davis ran for 102 yards against the Falcons for his seventh consecutive 100-yard postseason game to set a record. But this Super Bowl belonged to Elway. He knew before the game Atlanta's defense would build its game plan around trying to stop T.D. Elway took it as a slight. And aired it out. "Everybody talked about the running game all week," he said. "Anybody can stop the run if they put enough guys up on the line. I went in knowing I'd have the opportunity to throw the football...I was looking forward to the opportunity."

As a result, Elway took out his former coach (and quasi-nemesis) Reeves. "He's a great quarterback," Reeves said. "He doesn't have to apologize for anything. I thought he was a great quarterback when he lost three Super Bowls. I'm sure it puts a big smile on his face because he was the MVP, and they win back-to-back Super Bowls. That's hard to beat. The only thing that could beat that is three. He may come back to try for three."

He would not. Everyone wants to go out on top. The trick is to go out like Elway.

CHAPTER SIXTEEN

ELWAY, THE GM

On the top floor of the Jersey City Hyatt Regency, Denver Broncos executives, coaches, a few players, and staff employees had gathered for their post-Super Bowl XLVIII party. Party wasn't the correct word. The occasion more resembled a wake.

The Broncos were embarrassed again in losing a Super Bowl—this time 43–8 against the Seattle Seahawks on February 2, 2014, at MetLife Stadium, the gameday home of the New York Giants and Jets. At least when John Elway, the Broncos quarterback, met the Giants in Super Bowl XXI and Washington Redskins in Super Bowl XXII, Denver had an early lead. The queso and dip tasted good for a quarter or so. In this one against the Seahawks, the game was over from the first snap.

With far more New York City crowd noise than antic-ipated at a neutral-site Super Bowl, Broncos center Manny Ramirez didn't hear Peyton Manning audible the protection as the quarterback was moving up from his shotgun posi-tion. Ramirez snapped the ball too soon and too high over Manning's shoulder—much to the quarterback's surprise. The hike sailed past Manning and into the end zone for a safety.

The rout was on. It was 22–0 Seattle at halftime, then 29–0 after Percy Harvin returned the opening kickoff of the second half 87 yards for a touchdown, and 36–0 before the Broncos scored their only touchdown—a 14-yard pass from Manning to Demaryius Thomas.

Then at the postgame gathering of employees, Elway was somber, demoralized, every bit as humiliated as he was when he was part of three Super Bowl blowouts as a quarterback. But this time he was also angry. Nearly 25 years after his most ignominious defeats on a national stage, he had returned to a Super Bowl as a general manager, the Broncos' roster architect. *The Broncos can't just lose a Super Bowl. They have to always endure an embarrassing blowout?* This time Elway was fuming mad. Furious with his head coach John Fox for not having the team better prepared. Irked that Manning's record-setting passing season got carried away to the point the offense wasn't complimentary to the defense and therefore wasn't conducive to winning Super Bowls.

Elway knew the Air Peyton train was steaming dangerously down the track. But the Broncos were having so much fun setting records and beating overmatched opponents he couldn't advise against it. Manning had a 2013 season for the ages. He threw 55 touchdown passes to set a single-season record that still stands 11 years later, including the three seasons from 2021 to 2023 when the NFL had expanded its regular seasons from 16 to 17 games. Manning in 16 games also threw for 5,477 yards, another record. Even Manning thought his yardage record would last about two weeks, but here it is 10 years later, and no one has since approached it. The Broncos scored a record 606 points, again a mark still standing in NFL single-season annals for an incredible 37.9 points per game. And yet, the Broncos showed up in New York City to get obliterated in another Super Bowl.

In the Broncos' 15ᵗʰ regular-season game, which came against the Houston Texans, Manning broke Tom Brady's single-season record of 50 touchdown passes by throwing three touchdowns in the fourth quarter—his No. 49, 50, and 51 on the season. "I'll never forget," Elway said in November 2023. Manning added four more touchdown passes a week later against the Oakland Raiders in the season finale to pad his record.

The Broncos finished 13–3 and had the No. 1 AFC playoff seed for a second consecutive year and beat the San Diego Chargers and Brady's Patriots in the postseason to reach the first ever Super Bowl to be hosted by New York City. A snowstorm had crushed America's No. 1 largest city in the days before the Super Bowl festivities and again on the morning after. "I was happy for Peyton, but it was like all we tried to do now is throw touchdown passes," Elway said. "And that bothered me. So I was like, let's get out of this numbers game. We still have a good team, but we have to run the ball and do some different things. And then after we got busted by Seattle—it's funny I was with my nephew, Janet's son [Patrick Walsh]—and we were sitting there, and that was the night I was so mad, and I said, 'We're going to turn this around and go the other way. We're going to go defense' because I knew Peyton was [backsliding] a little bit, even though he was still Peyton."

In one of the most remarkable if unappreciated accomplishments in NFL general manager history, Elway over the course of three seasons, transferred the Broncos from the Showtime Lakers in reaching the Super Bowl in 2013 to the Bad Boy Pistons in winning the Super Bowl in 2015. Two completely different styles. Run-and-gun with Manning as the point guard and a remarkable set of skill-position weapons on his flanks in 2013. A blitzing, physical, Von Miller and DeMarcus Ware attacking, defensive-dominating team that overcame a struggling offense to win it all in 2015. "It all started that night after the Super Bowl," said Walsh, who was hired by the Broncos two years later as a personnel intern and has since worked six years as a pro scout. "That's when it flipped. He wanted to rebuild the defense. John was really impressed by Seattle's defense. He had studied them going into the game but was really struck by how good they were live. Between talking out loud, venting, and connecting the dots, he started articulating exactly what needs to happen in order to win a Super Bowl. We started talking about guys he wanted to bring in that night."

T.J. Ward was one of the first targets. Seattle strong safety Kam Chancellor had just delivered some big hits that set the tone in Super Bowl XLVIII, and Ward was a Pro Bowl strong safety coming off a big year with the Cleveland Browns. Elway was in on Minnesota Vikings pass rusher Jared Allen at the onset of free agency, but when the Dallas Cowboys released Ware for financial reasons, the target moved. A day into the 2014 free agency, Elway had signed Ware, corner-back Aqib Talib, and Ward. A couple days later, the Broncos signed Pittsburgh Steelers receiver Emmanuel Sanders and the Broncos had what turned out to be the greatest free-agent class in franchise history.

Manning still had a little more half season of greatness in him in 2014 as he continued to break records, but following a 22–7 loss at the St. Louis Rams in Game 10, in which Manning threw it 54 times—56 counting his two sacks—against just nine rushing attempts, Elway stepped in from upstairs and ordered greater offensive balance. The Broncos were upset at home by Andrew Luck, Manning's successor as Indianapolis Colts quarterback, in a second-round playoff game after which Fox resigned while Elway held the door open for him. Elway then hired his good friend Gary Kubiak as head coach. Besides his great run with the Broncos in a previous life as Elway's backup quarterback and offensive coordinator, Kubiak had a mostly successful run as head coach with the Houston Texans from 2006 to 2013. Wade Phillips came back as Denver's defensive coordinator, and the Broncos wound up winning their third Super Bowl to cap 2015.

Miller and Ware were the key defenders in an AFC Championship Game home win against Brady and the Patriots, and Miller had two strip sack fumbles that led to two touchdowns in a 24–10 win against the Carolina Panthers in Super Bowl 50. There was talk of Canton, Ohio, commissioning a second bust for Elway—this time with a suit and tie neckline for his work as general manager.

The next five years in Elway's term, though, didn't go well. Manning retired after that Super Bowl win—he had just nine touchdown passes against 17 interceptions in his final regular season before putting together one more great run in the postseason. While starting second-year, seventh-round quarterback Trevor Siemian, the Broncos began 4–0 in 2016 thanks to their great defense. But Kubiak suffered his second TIA (transient ischemic attack or mini-stroke) following a Week Five loss to the Atlanta Falcons and he would retire from the head coaching business after that season. Without Kubiak to develop 2016 first-round pick Paxton Lynch, the Broncos struggled to find a quarterback.

The team missed the playoffs all five years and had losing seasons in the final four seasons under Elway, who retired as GM following the 2020 season. So his executive term was split right down the middle—terrific his first five years when the Broncos won five consecutive AFC West titles, including the first with Tim Tebow as his quarterback—and disappointing in his final five years when the team never reached the postseason. "Getting Peyton, we had some good years and we had some good drafts," Elway said. "Fox did a great job, but I felt we were stuck with where we were. So I hired Gary. Gary was a really good coach, but after he got sick, it was really tough finding that next guy who was in line with what I knew, what I liked. I kind of look back on it now. My mentality as a GM was to compete every year for Super Bowls. I should have been a little more longer-sighted and said, 'Okay, let's take our time. Let's build this thing right instead of trying to win a Super Bowl every year.' I was a little shortsighted because that's how I was a player, too. All I thought about was winning Super Bowls."

* * *

John Elway did announce his retirement as the Denver Broncos quarterback three months after his Super Bowl XXXIII MVP performance in Miami. Even though Elway had announced prior to that Super Bowl-winning season that he was 99.9 percent sure it would be his last season, some of his prominent teammates didn't think he would actually go through with it.

That includes left guard Mark Schlereth, who said he had no inclination Elway was about to play his last game. "No, because we were playing at a real high level," Schlereth said. "And even though John missed the majority of six games with that hamstring, he was still playing really well. It's hard to walk away when you're playing really well. But I also under-stand the concept of—it's not Sundays that make one retired. It's Mondays through Saturday that you don't want to do anymore. Even as a player, I didn't see what John had to do Monday through Saturday to get ready to play, and that does take its toll on you, man. It just wears you out physically and mentally."

Rod Smith, Elway's top receiver his final two seasons, was also surprised Elway retired. "I thought he was coming back," Smith said. "I was going to his press conference when I heard he retired. I was dumbfounded, upset, happy, sad—I had all the emotions that day because I really believed we had a core group of guys who would come back. The salary cap was going to be an issue. It always was, but I really thought he would come back and go for three. I really did. And then all the sudden, they tell us there's going to be a press conference about John supposedly retiring. I was in shock and I was very upset for selfish reasons. I was selfish. I learned so much from him my rookie year in how he approached the game. John would have all these appearances that would pay him $100,000, but he had in his contracts he could adjust it so he could attend the offseason program. I went to 600 straight offseason practices. I would have $10,000 for an appearance. If it interfered with my offseason practice, I would say no. I followed John's lead on that. I really wanted him to come back, and the wheels completely fell off the next year."

Indeed, without Elway, Mike Shanahan's Broncos started 0–4. Worse, Terrell Davis suffered a season-ending knee injury while chasing down an interception return in that fourth loss. As it turned out, it can be said Davis suffered a career-ending knee injury. He did return for three more years but was never the same. "We had some decent running backs behind him," Smith said. "But they weren't T.D."

Davis said he was disappointed with Elway's decision to retire but understood it more with each subsequent year as he went through his own physical travails. "Believe me: my thought was, *I wish we could try it one more time*," Davis said in November 2023. "But because I know how it was, having to miss practice, having to be on stem and the trainer's room and can barely to make it to practice. He's fighting just to prepare for a game physically. That takes a toll that's hard to imagine unless you're going through it. I went through it and, when I started going through it, I remember thinking of John retiring and I was like, 'I understand.' You were fighting an uphill battle to just to be even par, not even to be great. I'm not training to be superior in strength. I'm training to be equal in strength. I'm so beat up from a physical standpoint I'm barely on par with myself. *And I'm trying to go on and be great?* The math just doesn't add up. I wish he would have just waited. Everyone after the season thinks, *I'm done.* The body just seeks relief. You're just ready to be done with it. But, hey, I respect his decision, but there's always that, what if?"

Nearly 25 years later, Elway was told about how his teammates were surprised he retired. Clearly, he didn't tell them about his decision until he announced his retirement to the media and fans at an emotional press conference. "No, because I wasn't positive," Elway said. "I did it saying I would get far enough away and have time to think about it. The thing that happened was Bubby [Brister] played well when I got hurt that year."

Yes, he said 25 years later, he probably could have played one more season. But even his dad communicated doubt as to whether he should. "After the second Super Bowl, my dad said, 'John you can still play, but it's a matter whether you want to go through all that,'" Elway recalled. "I was getting tired of all the media stuff. And then when you're 38 and the locker room is now 15 years younger, you feel like you've been there long enough. I kind of was looking forward to having some more time, too."

He went out on top and doubled it. Back-to-back happy endings for The Duke. A year later Broncos owner Pat Bowlen did try to sell Elway a 10 percent slice of the team, but the move was blocked by the team's previous owner Edgar Kaiser Jr., who had a right-of-first-refusal clause when he sold the team to Bowlen. The matter got hung up in courts, and though Bowlen eventually prevailed, the 10 percent sale to Elway never materialized.

Elway's legacy was secure. He was one of the greatest quarterbacks of all time and one of the winningest. He was the greatest player in Broncos history and he finished with back-to-back Super Bowl titles. His pristine legacy, though, was no match for the powerful need to compete that continued to burn inside long after his body no longer allowed him to play.

He risked that sterling legacy all by taking up Bowlen on his offer to become the Broncos general manager in 2011. It was a huge risk to Elway's sterling biography because GMs almost always eventually get fired. The best-laid plans don't work out. "Lot of things are out of your control," Elway said. "But ultimately it's what I wanted to do. And that's why I did the Arena team. I got some experience doing that and I enjoyed doing that."

The Colorado Crush won the Arena League championship in 2005. Elway was the Crush's GM. But building an NFL roster added multiple more levels of competitiveness and pressure. Legacy, schmegacy, Elway wanted to compete. And he proved all his life he loved performing under pressure. Plus, he didn't really want to run for a political office, as his Republican party tried to lure him into several times. His car dealerships made money, but then what? *Sit around and count it?* He was a very good golfer but not quite good enough to make a serious go on the PGA Tour.

The Broncos had struggled without him. It was 2011 when Bowlen talked to Elway and his wife, Paige, over dinner about coming back to run the Broncos' football operations. The Broncos had fired head coach and football operations boss Josh McDaniels. Denver was 4–12 in 2010, its 12th consecutive year without a Super Bowl appearance.

The Broncos needed Elway, and then 12 years since his retirement, Elway wanted them.

"I always wanted to come back in some capacity whatever that may be," Elway said. "I didn't want to coach. My dad did it, and all that time it requires, I didn't want to do that. So to come back as general manager, I had seen it and knew what it takes. I'd been there and I knew what it takes to win and to win a Super Bowl. So I wanted a crack at running a football team and being part of the decision-making process. I had seen teams that had lost Super Bowls, teams that had won Super Bowls. Going through seasons how you win it, the type of coaches I wanted."

His first five years as GM brought five AFC West titles, two Super Bowls, and one Lombardi Trophy. The next five years brought none of that. "The end of the tenure didn't end well," said Schlereth, who became an ESPN analyst and morning host on a Denver sports talk radio station, 104.3 The Fan. He was sometimes critical of Elway during the final years of his GM term. "On the radio I'm always going to be honest, but sometimes you don't say it as eloquently as you should. That being said, he'll always be the Duke of Denver. He'll always be the Godfather. Let's not forget they did happen to go to two world championships and won one in his tenure. There's a lot of GMs who would switch positions right now so I think that will soften over time. The other thing you can't take for granted that we all take for granted, and that's there was no ownership. If your ownership isn't correct and the system of checks and balances isn't right, it's impossible to win. I know the Trust did the best they could. But that's a really sticky situation. You've got have somebody in charge. And you're the GM and in charge of all things football, and there's no system of checks and balances there."

Bowlen's hiring of Elway late in the 2010 season was the last critical decision he made before the ravages of Alzheimer's disease took over. Joe Ellis, as president, CEO, and owner delegee, and Elway were in charge of the team from 2011 to 2015, when the Broncos were historically successful. But when the team slumped after Super Bowl 50, not having an owner was often blamed. "The other regret was I passed on Josh Allen because I liked him," Elway said about his 2018 decision to take defensive end Bradley Chubb with the Broncos' No. 5 overall draft selection instead of the Wyoming quarterback. "But I couldn't get the coaching staff to buy in at all. That's the one thing I wish I would have gone with what I felt was right. Athletic, move around. Not real accurate, that was his only negative coming out, but he could make all the throws, strong arm. I could not get the staff to buy in."

Allen became the No. 7 overall selection of the Buffalo Bills, where he has accumulated terrific passing and rushing numbers. But he's still looking for his first Super Bowl appearance.

Despite the struggles of the final half of his GM tenure, Elway remains the most impactful person in Broncos' history. The body of great work—16 years as a quarterback, 10 years as GM, seven Super Bowl appearances, three Lombardi Trophies— easily absorbed five losing seasons as GM. "We absolutely do not win two Super Bowls without John Elway," said receiver

Ed McCaffrey. "In the front office, he went on to win another one. He has meant so much to this organization as one of the greatest players to ever play in the history of the NFL and certainly the greatest player in Broncos history. But then he topped it by going into the front office and helping to bring Peyton Manning to Denver and winning another Super Bowl. His impact has been monumental."

Six-time Pro Bowler Karl Mecklenburg, who played linebacker/defensive end for the Broncos from 1983 to 1994, summed it up best: "He definitely was the most influential and impactful person for the franchise," he said. "He was in the middle of seven of the eight Super Bowls."

ACKNOWLEDGMENTS

No one can undertake this type of historical project alone.

First and foremost, gratitude to John Elway. I've sat him down for multiple Broncos book projects in the past. So I wasn't sure he would want to again. How many times does a man have to retell the story about The Drive? But he did, and this book would not have been nearly as good without our interview over a late breakfast at Perfect Landing restaurant before he was to fly out of Centennial Airport.

To Elway's teammates during the Broncos' back-to-back Super Bowl seasons of 1997–98: Terrell Davis, Mark Schlereth, Ed McCaffrey, Rod Smith, Jason Elam, Bill Romanowski, Vaughn Hebron, Mike Lodish.

To Elway's teammates during the three Super Bowl appearances of the Dan Reeves era: Karl Mecklenburg, Steve Watson, and Mark Jackson.

To the players from the Orange Crush era who welcomed Elway to Denver with open arms, not jealousy: Tom Jackson, Steve Foley, and Barney Chavous.

To coaches Mike Shanahan and Gary Kubiak. Shanahan held our two lengthy conversations—first the meat of the book, then for the foreword—at the popular Denver Tech Center steakhouse that bears his name. Put that man in the Pro Football Hall of Fame and Kubiak in the Broncos' Ring of Fame.

To Broncos public relations assistant Erich Shubert, who dug up all the old box scores that were otherwise difficult to find.

To Jim Saccomano, who was available to answer a historical question at moment's notice.

To my 9NEWS boss Brian Olson and teammates Johnny Kuhrt, Jeff Dressel, Scotty Gange, Arielle Orsuto and Jacob Tobey.

To Bill Ames of Triumph, who came up with this book idea, and Jeff Fedotin, my editor.

And, finally, to my wife, Becky, who if she said it once, she said it a hundred times: "Why don't you go upstairs and work on your book."

SOURCES

Through the JeffersonCoLibrary.com, I was able to go through NewsBank, which offered the three big Colorado newspapers:

The Denver Post (1989–current)
Colorado Springs Gazette-Telegraph (1988–current)
Rocky Mountain News (1990–2009)

Those three newspapers were invaluable resources for John Elway's final years—in particular the Super Bowl-winning seasons of 1997–98 and the 1996 season that led up to those back-to-back titles.

Also:

9NEWS.com for Broncos stories since the 2015 NFL Draft written by Mike Klis

Elway, A Relentless Life by Jason Cole and Hachette Book Group

The 50 Greatest Players in Denver Broncos History by Mike Klis and Lyons Press

The Denver Broncos All-Time All-Stars by Mike Klis and The Rowman & Littlefield Publishing Group, Inc.